CONVERSATION AS METHOD

CONVERSATION AS METHOD

Analyzing the
Relational World of
People Who
Were Raised
Communally

Ruthellen Josselson
Amia Lieblich
Ruth Sharabany
Hadas Wiseman

(in alphabetical order)

SAGE Publications
International Educational and Professional Publisher
Thousand Oaks London New Delhi

Copyright © 1997 by Sage Publications, Inc.

All rights reserved. No part of this book may be reproduced or utilized in any form or by any means, electronic or mechanical, including photocopying, recording, or by any information storage and retrieval system, without permission in writing from the publisher.

For information:

SAGE Publications, Inc.
2455 Teller Road
Thousand Oaks, California 91320
E-mail: order@sagepub.com

SAGE Publications Ltd.
6 Bonhill Street
London EC2A 4PU
United Kingdom

SAGE Publications India Pvt. Ltd.
M-32 Market
Greater Kailash I
New Delhi 110 048 India

Printed in the United States of America

Library of Congress Cataloging-in-Publication Data

Conversation as method: Analyzing the relational world of people who were raised communally / by Ruthellen Josselson ... [et al.].
    p. cm.
    Includes bibliographical references (p.) and index.
    ISBN 0-7619-0512-X (cloth: acid-free paper). —
ISBN 0-7619-0513-8 (pbk.: acid-free paper)
    1. Kibbutzim—Psychological aspect. 2. Socialization—Israel.
3. Interpersonal relations—Israel. I. Josselson, Ruthellen.
HX742.2.A3C67 1997
307.77'6—dc21   97-4674

This book is printed on acid-free paper.

97 98 99 00 01 02 03 10 9 8 7 6 5 4 3 2 1

Acquiring Editor:	C. Terry Hendrix
Editorial Assistant:	Dale Grenfell
Production Editor:	Sanford Robinson
Production Assistant:	Denise Santoyo
Book Designer/Typesetter:	Janelle LeMaster
Cover Designer:	Ravi Balasuriya
Print Buyer:	Anna Chin

CONTENTS

Prologue	vii
1. How Does Growing Up Communally Affect Relationships? *Ruth Sharabany* and *Hadas Wiseman*	1
2. Eight Dimensions of Relationship *Ruthellen Josselson*	13
3. The Dialogue Begins	21
4. Holding	31
5. Attachment	43
6. Passions	59
7. Eye-to-Eye Validation	73
8. Idealization and Identification	89
9. Mutuality and Resonance	101
10. Embeddedness	113
11. Tending (Care)	123
12. Reflections on the Discourse	135
References	154
Index	159
About the Authors	167

PROLOGUE

Feminist approaches to research (Reinharz, 1992) and other postmodern scientific methods begin with the assumption that there is no single truth and no unique research procedure that suffices for the production of knowledge. In the past, science has largely been conducted by scholars working individually trying to refute, subsume, or supplant each other's position and promulgate their own presumably superior theory. By focusing on the importance of collaborative paths to knowledge, the postmodern and feminist critique has legitimated scholars working together, despite diversity, to collectively explore understanding.

Beyond working together as scholars, feminist researchers have sought to involve their participants actively in the search for understanding. Often using the interview as a primary means of data gathering, feminist researchers draw on their participants' view of reality to generate theory. Raw material is drawn from the participants' own words, and voice is honored rather than masked. The outcome of this process is a set of understandings that may or may not evolve into theory. Scholarly knowing comes closer to phenomenological experience.

But, in the absence of a repeatable "method," it is often hard to know how universally applicable one's observations may be or how to generalize from individual cases. The standard procedure for presenting research has been to avoid the first-person singular as though there is no knower and to eliminate reference to the actual people who inform our knowing. The feminist position is that knowledge is co-constructed by observer and observed and that both must be clearly visible in research reports. The method of this book is to bring together researchers, all women, all interested in feminist methodology, all of whom have worked independently on the same topic, and to develop among ourselves a conversation about phenomena that we have all studied from somewhat different points of view. Unlike the blind men and the elephant, we fully recognize that we are observing from different angles, and we try together to construct the whole beast. We hope, through our collaboration, to build a collective story. Our presentation of this material is radical but fully in line with the spirit of new approaches to methodology. Rather than resolve our differences and present our digested compromises in an expert authorial voice, we make public our process of thinking about our material and thereby explore multiple perspectives on a multilayered topic. The interconnection between who we are and what we know is apparent rather than veiled. And the reader is free to observe the intersection of the multiple truths we encounter—and how we attempt to integrate them.

We bring diverse approaches into the dialogue. Two of us have worked qualitatively, one has used only quantitative methods, and the fourth combined both. We may explore together our different ways of knowing. How do the case studies amplify, illuminate, or contradict the statistical evidence? How can we understand the different impressions each of us may have derived from our interviews? Is there something "out there" that each of us, with our differing vision, sees? Or are we just seeing ourselves and the shadows of our methods? We believe that this research conversation, beyond what we explore in the topic of our work, goes to the core of epistemology. As we talk together about our work, we are thinking about our own process in constructing knowledge. Good social science evolves from people coming together to talk and listen and learn from one another. Conversation makes more demands than a single authorial voice. In effect, we invite our readers to join our conversation and make their own judgments on our differences. We hope that the process of witnessing and containing those differences will enrich our readers as well.

HOW DOES GROWING UP COMMUNALLY AFFECT RELATIONSHIPS?

RUTH SHARABANY
HADAS WISEMAN

We have noted, through our experiences as developmental researchers, that psychological theories of human development begin from the premise that the normative mode of human growth is the nuclear, two-parent family. But children are increasingly being raised in alternate situations. As psychologists, we need to understand better what are the necessary emotional ingredients provided by the family and how parenting fits into the larger society. Usually, when we observe people raised in other structures, it is the result of trauma or social disruption. Death of a parent, divorce, social dislocation that creates orphans, family abuse—all these may necessitate children being raised outside the home. But when we bring to these structures questions about their effects on children, it is difficult to sort out what is the effect of trauma, what is compensatory, and what is generally growth-producing in the child's environment. Rarely has there been an opportunity to study people raised in social organizations other than the nuclear family where the social structure was created by design and intention.

Psychological theory further traces all adult relationships to the early patterning of relationships with parents. But what happens to people who are raised other than in a home with parents? How are their later relationships affected? Relationships and the capacity to form them are much affected by context, both early and current. By studying people whose early development diverged from the "ordinary" path, not because of trauma or social disruption, we hoped we could better understand the critical ingredients of the early child-parent interaction and their later effects. The Israeli kibbutz provides such an opportunity: Among other things, it has been a system of communal child-rearing that grew from ideology rather than social disruption. The kibbutz has been a focus of interest for social scientists for decades now. The kibbutz offered a naturalistic social experiment: In a modern Western industrial society of middle-class people, children were raised apart from their parents in a peer group from the day they are born. By the mid-1990s, this social experiment had changed so much that it is no longer available as a laboratory for investigation of these questions. Therefore, the time is right to try to piece together what we, as psychologists, have learned from what took place.

STUDYING THE EFFECTS OF COMMUNAL CHILD-RAISING IN THE KIBBUTZ

Since their establishment in the beginning of the 20th century, the normal practice in the kibbutzim has been to put offspring of kibbutz members first into infant homes in groups of four to six babies cared for by a semiprofessional woman known as a *metapelet*. Mothers were allowed and in later years encouraged to breast-feed or to come for feeding, but other than that, all the caregiving was done by the metapelet and within the peer group. Parents took care of their children for 2-3 hours each afternoon, hours called the "loving hours." Children returned to the children's houses for the night. The children's houses were designed for a child's needs, with special areas for sleeping, eating, studying, and playing. Extracurricular activities, such as music, arts and crafts, and sports, were provided. The community saw education as a priority and allocated its best human and economic resources to the goal of communal upbringing. But the essential features of this upbringing were the separation from parents (and siblings) and the peer group experience from the beginning of life onward (see Bettelheim, 1969; Rabin & Beit-Hallahmi, 1982).

Within psychology alone, many researchers tried to study the impact of this unique sociological structure on a variety of outcomes (Beit-Hallahmi & Rabin, 1977). The array of questions that have been asked ranged from what level of intelligence, creativity, and moral judgment has been achieved by kibbutz-raised children, to what degree of cooperation, intimacy, and emotional expression has been possible for them (e.g., Regev, Beit-Hallahmi, & Sharabany, 1980). Does this special kind of upbringing promote or hinder the relationships children could or would form with others? For example, what are the effects on infant development of early exposure to multiple caregivers in the context of group care? Could the communal structure of child-rearing serve as a buffer against mental breakdown, which is predicted by heredity, such as in schizophrenia (Nathan, Frenkel, & Kugelmas, 1993)? Are kibbutz-raised children more extroverted, more dependent on others? Or the opposite—would they become saturated with people and crave privacy? Is there a "kibbutz personality" (Rabin, 1957)? Is this personality effective and well-adjusted, or are there pathological features (Rabin & Beit- Hallahmi, 1982)? A major concern that grew out of this research was that people would be disturbed in their relationships (Berman, 1988) as a result of not having the same close intimate ties with parents as children who lived with their parents and slept under the same roof. Bettelheim (1969), in the 6 weeks he spent studying the kibbutz, came away convinced that people raised in this way were hampered in forming intimate relationships. Others, however, have shown that there is little empirical evidence for such impairment.

Did the communal child-rearing help or hurt people? The evidence was unclear. Much of the early research in this area was done in a context of intense debate, in which research findings became grist for the ideological mill. Research was conducted in an emotion-laden climate, a tug of war between those trying to prove the kibbutz experience was not harmful and those fearful that it might prove to be so. The kibbutz is no longer as collective in its approaches to child care; thus, the commitment to this past system has waned. Research no longer entails recommendations or takes ideological sides. It is perhaps a better time to try to learn from what occurred in order to inform our understanding of human development rather than to reform social practice. Psychology has not yet fully reaped the harvest of what was, in effect, an enormous social experimental laboratory.

THE REALITIES OF DAILY LIFE IN THE KIBBUTZ

Although the fact of sleeping in a children's house rather than with one's parents was the most visible social change wrought by the kibbutz, the ideology of the collective, in fact, permeated all other aspects of life as well. Socialist values dictated equality and direct democracy, with all adult members of the community having equal impact on decision-making processes. Formally, women have the same status as men, and the kibbutz structure freed women from everyday household tasks by providing communal solutions to cooking, laundry, and so on. However, in practice, women were most often assigned to traditionally feminine roles almost exclusively (Swirski & Safir, 1991; Talmon-Garber, 1972)—in child care, education, and other services.

Because the kibbutz community took over most of the maintenance function of the family, there should have been more time and energy for high-quality activities between parents and children and between the members of the couple. Men were not under the pressure of "making a living," and their work was done close to where the family lived, so that fathers and children could interact more during the day. The cultural life of the family was interwoven in community life. Holidays were celebrated in the community, with children taking part. Adults and children lived well—in middle-class conditions, with all reasonable material needs satisfied and comprehensive health care provided.

Changes in child care practices have resulted from national changes in political security and economic conditions as well as a general disillusionment with the communal way of life; this disillusionment is the outcome of the frequent conflict between the needs of the community and the wishes of the individual. One implication of communal life, for example, was the requirement that the individual follow communal decision making even in very personal matters, such as study programs, jobs, or vacations. For example, parents were not allowed to make educational decisions for their children—the community decided where the child would go to school and adjudicated conflicts with teachers or metapelets. Paradoxically, although the ideological base of the kibbutz was a source of closeness and similarity among members, it was also a source of fierce personal battles regarding details of actual decisions.

RESEARCH ON KIBBUTZ-REARED CHILDREN: AN OVERVIEW

In reviewing the research literature on the effect of socialization on kibbutz-reared children, it is evident that the questions addressed reflect the paradigms and theoretical frameworks in developmental psychology of the time. The first paradigm, following World War II and the institutionalization of orphans, addressed the issue of the syndrome of hospitalism—that is, the result of raising children in institutions. The documented detrimental consequences of institutionalization to the mental health and development of children generated studies that focused on normality versus psychopathology in kibbutz children. In this paradigm, the kibbutz was used as a case of growing up in "institutional care" without the adverse conditions of orphanhood and war. Did the kibbutz-reared children suffer from *maternal deprivation*, with detrimental effects similar to the "hospitalism syndrome" (Spiro, 1958)? Studies of infants in the kibbutz showed no evidence of either retardation or emotional disorders (e.g., Fried, 1960). Moreover, the pattern of smiling among the kibbutz-born was more like that of home-reared children than that of either institutionalized or day nursery children (Gewirtz, 1965).

The second framework was that of *maternal substitution*. Because the various roles of the mother were delegated to other adults in the community, the question was how children would view their mothers as well as other adults. The role of parents in the two central dimensions of support and discipline was compared for city children, children raised in a *moshav* (where there is some communal sharing, but children are raised in the family home), and children raised communally in the kibbutz. Kibbutz parents were found to maintain their role of support, yet the disciplinary role was delegated to the metapelet (Avgar, Bronfenbrenner, & Henderson, 1977; Devereux et al., 1974). Furthermore, the mother in the kibbutz retained her role as the first person children said they would turn to for help, support, and so on. Clearly, the kibbutz was in no way a depriving environment. The mother retained her significance. The issue became one of considering the implications of multiple mothering for the kibbutz child's interpersonal development.

The third, most recent paradigm is the focus on attachment patterns. Bowlby's (1969/1982) attachment theory assumed that early attachment relationships with caregivers provide the prototype for later social relations. He based his initial theory implicitly on the mother-child relationship in the context of the traditional nuclear Western family. Investigating attachment patterns in the kibbutz provided the opportunity to extend and elaborate on Bowlby's theory beyond the nuclear family structure (Fox, 1977; Maccoby & Feldman, 1972). Using Ainsworth, Blehar, Waters, and Wall's (1978) strange situation paradigm, communally raised babies were compared to city-raised babies. The specific pattern that seemed to predominate in the communally raised babies was that of insecure attachment (Oppenheim, Sagi, & Lamb, 1988; Sagi et al., 1985). The prevalence of the insecure-ambivalent pattern was related to communal sleeping arrangements and was more common among these infants than those who were raised on a kibbutz but lived with their parents (Sagi, Van Ijzendoorn, Aviezer, Donnell, & Mayseless, 1994). But researchers debated over how to interpret the results. Perhaps the communally raised children were more sensitive to separation from their parents and hence protested more.

Close Relationships

Other research used objective measures to assess aspects of close relationships among communally raised people after they were beyond the stage of infancy and childhood (reviewed in Sharabany & Wiseman, 1993; in press). Compared to city children of the same age, preadolescent children raised in the kibbutz reported being less intimate with their best friends on several aspects of intimacy. Although they reported doing more activities with their best friends, they were less open and communicative with them and reported less trust and less exclusiveness in the relationship (Sharabany, 1974). This study was replicated, comparing family-raised with communally raised children reared in the kibbutz (Arnon, 1978); the intimacy of family-raised kibbutz children was more like that of city children.

Studies on self-disclosure found that although adolescents in the kibbutz viewed self-disclosing as desirable and positive, just as much as their city counterparts did, they nevertheless self-disclosed to a lesser extent than city adolescents. Moreover, they used less emotion in their indirect expressions as well as in direct expressions. Examining the stories they told on a projective TAT test revealed that they depicted less emotion (Biran, 1983). Kibbutz children in the communal sleeping arrangement chose more often to avoid expression of feelings, both negative and positive, compared to both kibbutz children in the family sleeping arrangement and children raised in the city. On other tests, they showed relatively more negative feelings toward teachers and peers, as well as less negative emotion toward parents and siblings. The picture that emerges is of communally raised adolescents being more guarded about their feelings, less available for intimacy than those who were raised in nuclear families.

In contrast to the findings on preadolescents and adolescents, married couples in the kibbutz did not differ from city couples on a measure of intimacy with their spouses (Hershlag, 1984). With the high prevalence of marital breakup ending in divorce in the United States, and the evidence of low rates of marital stability in many American communes, social researchers have been interested in the frequency of divorce in the kibbutz. Compared to the city, the kibbutz offered favorable conditions for divorce, in that both husband and wife were assured continued economic security and equal opportunities for co-parenting, thus reducing fears of disruption in daily contact with children. In spite of the relatively more conducive conditions for divorce in the kibbutz, data from the 1970s showed a lower rate of divorce in the kibbutz than in the larger cities in Israel. In recent years, however, when the kibbutz has become more familial in its structure and less communal at the same time that formal and informal social controls were loosened, there has been a marked tendency toward a rise in the rate of divorce in the kibbutz (Kaffman, Shoham, & Elizur, 1986). This raises many interesting questions regarding expectations about marriage and its place in the life of men and women, while taking into consideration the specific context of the community and its values and norms.

Finally, in regard to the process of aging, the kibbutz is unique in that it provides its elderly members with complete care within the kibbutz environment. In the kibbutz, the care of frail elderly members is recognized as a public responsibility, consistent with the kibbutz ethos and structure. Studies on impaired elderly people in Israeli kibbutzim have shown that despite the unlimited availability of formal resources, informal supports continue to play a major role. Moreover, lack of informal caregivers emerged as an important risk factor for institutionalization, even in the service-rich environment of kibbutzim (Holmes, 1989; Teresi, 1989). Hence, even within this close-knit community, those having kin in the kibbutz are at an advantage. No wonder that parents are interested in having at least one son or daughter who will stay in the kibbutz to complement the care of the kibbutz in old age.

Research to date, then, has not demonstrated a clear detrimental effect of the communal sleeping arrangement, whether in short-term or long-term follow-ups. The effects of this experience are unclear, and most research has been based on measures that might not be sensitive to some of the subtle psychological effects.

The Relational Prism

Our interest in how communally based "working models" of relationship would play out later in life coincided with psychology's movement from a preoccupation with autonomy and separation to an interest in the growth and differentiation of relationships. We began to wonder if perhaps relationships among communally raised people were not equally affected in all their aspects. If we think of relatedness in a complex way, some aspects of relationship may be highlighted whereas other parts go in the shadow. In the kibbutz, for example, there are built-in tensions (as in all societies) between belonging and individuation. It may well be that people sacrifice their experience of personal validation with others in order to reap the feeling of embeddedness with them. Perhaps sharing and self-revelation are minimized in order to safeguard attachments. But to explore these questions, we must work with a broad-based differentiated model of relatedness, one close to experience, and listen to how communally raised people speak of how their interpersonal life developed. In the next chapter, we describe an eight-dimension model of relationships, a model we have agreed to use together. It will serve as a prism through which we look at what our research participants have told us—each of us independently, working in different paradigms at different times—about growing up communally in the kibbutz. Together we reflect on what this may imply for the study of early development and its effects on human relationship.

OUR METHODOLOGIES

To the conversation that follows, then, each of us brings understandings gleaned from different methods of approaching our shared question. Ruthellen Josselson used a relational mapping technique as a basis for intensive interviews that focused on a retrospective account of who had been important in each participant's life and, specifically, how those people had mattered and been emotionally significant. As a part of a larger study to define the space of relational experience, Ruthellen interviewed 120 people, of whom 16 had been raised communally on a kibbutz. Of these, 8 left the kibbutz as adults whereas 8 remained. All interviews lasted 3 to 5 hours.

Amia Lieblich conducted a long field research project in one Israeli kibbutz in 1978. The research involved open interviews with more than 100 members, and the outcome was reported in a book called *Kibbutz Makom* (Lieblich, 1981), written in the oral history tradition. After the publication of this study in Hebrew and English, Amia became involved in many consultations in different kibbutzim. Her continuous relationship with Kibbutz Makom (a pseudonym) was recently described (Lieblich, 1996). In addition to this in-depth study, Amia participated with Hadas Wiseman in a study on loneliness in the kibbutz (Wiseman & Lieblich, 1992), especially in the analysis of the narrative material collected by Hadas. Currently, Amia is conducting a new study in a young kibbutz that may be moved from its location in the Jordan Valley as part of the Israeli-Arab peace process. Finally, in her role as a group therapist, she has frequently encountered ex-kibbutz members in groups and thus had the chance to learn about their experiences on a deeper level. To sum up, Amia's research interests in the kibbutz have a long history, and they have always used rather unstructured, in-depth interviews for the data-gathering phase.

Ruth Sharabany's personal contact with the Israeli kibbutz was through the youth movement, typical of many youth of her generation in Israel. The youth movement provided years of contact with the kibbutz. A central part of the ideology was to join the kibbutz, thus fulfilling socialist and nationalist values. The kibbutz was looked up to as a society that was not based on materialistic and personal goals, but rather aspired to social fairness, a society whose members set national and international values above their own, sacrificing in meaningful ways toward these goals. It is with great respect for their efforts and appreciation of their contribution to Israeli society that Sharabany views kibbutz society to this day. Many of her studies deal with the personal lives of those who engaged in communal living.

Ruth's involvement in research on the kibbutz began in 1968, when a large-scale study of socialization in the kibbutz was initiated by Urie Bronfenbrenner as part of his cross-cultural studies on child development with colleagues at Cornell University and as a continuation of his study of Soviet education and its communal ideology. The kibbutz was viewed not only as another cultural variation, but rather as an "experiment in ecology," foreshadowing the development of Bronfenbrenner's strong commitment to an ecological perspective. The Israeli team included Ron Shuval and the late Moshe Rib and Sophie Kav Venaki, who directed the Israeli end of the collaboration between the University of Tel Aviv and Cornell University. Outstanding psychologists who were also kibbutz members served as consultants to the project—Michael Nathan and the late Menachem Gerson. After participating in the project's design and the first part of data collection, Ruth continued her involvement at the Cornell end in 1969. Several additional stages occurred there, including a large-scale data collection from many kibbutzim sampled from all over the country. Many different aspects of kibbutz socialization were studied, and only some of them published (e.g., Shuval et al., 1975); they are cited in our conversation.

At Cornell University, Ruth developed a special focus on intimate friendship among kibbutz children. At the time, quantitative studies of intimacy and friendship in general were rare. This work resulted in her doctoral dissertation, as well as a comprehensive bibliography on socialization in the kibbutz (Sharabany, 1974).

Since 1975, Ruth has supervised (with colleagues) many studies on the kibbutz, mostly as work on graduate theses at the University of Haifa and Tel Aviv University. The areas covered relate to development of moral judgment (Toren, 1979); intimate relations of adolescent girls with parents and friends (Yariv, 1983); longitudinal follow-up of the development of intimate friendships (Lev-Ran, 1980); expression of emotions by children in various sleeping arrangements (Arnon, 1978; Regev, 1976); relations between comradeship and intimate friendship (Rosenthal, 1980); relations in the kibbutz with parents, spouses, and friends (Dana-Engelstein, 1978; Kaminer, 1979). Most recently, she and her students have been studying attachment patterns of mothers who were raised on kibbutzim in family versus communal sleeping arrangements and are currently raising their children under similar or different conditions (Edry, 1995; Fuchs, 1995; Lulav, 1994).

Hadas Wiseman conducted a study on kibbutz-born young adults that focused on individuation and close relationships. She was interested in how the context of growing up in the kibbutz would influence the processes of separation and individuation, the achievement of intimacy, and the experience of loneliness during the transition to adulthood. Leaving home, in the context of the kibbutz, has an added meaning; for the young adult, leaving the parents' home may often mean leaving the parents' way of life (unless one moves to another kibbutz). Therefore, her study included young adults who were single, half of them living in the kibbutz and the other half living outside the kibbutz (i.e., away from home). The methodology she employed included both questionnaire data of a sample of about 100 respondents and data from interviews she conducted with about 50 people. In collaboration with Amia Lieblich, Hadas had the interviews transcribed and then carried out a content analysis of themes and categories, leading to construction of a tripartite representation referring to the kibbutz, others, and the self (Wiseman & Lieblich, 1992).

Together, then, we have viewed our questions through different methodological lenses, but our questions have had much in common. For this conversation, we agree on a common vocabulary and prism and then attempt to find out what we can know together.

2 EIGHT DIMENSIONS OF RELATIONSHIP

RUTHELLEN JOSSELSON

Here I present a model of relationship that my colleagues have agreed to use to frame our conversation. I developed this model because I had become increasingly aware that psychology understands the self far better than it understands connections between people. Whereas we have a useful theory of internal life, we most often talk about relations between people by encasing them in the language of psychopathology. Needing support from another gets defined as *dependence;* worrying about another's well-being is a symptom of *codependence.*

We have in our lexicon relatively few words to talk about our vast experience with relationship. There is an ancient holy Hindu book that says humankind knows only one quarter of all the speech that exists. Reality, then, far exceeds what we can express. We simply don't have enough language to encompass what we know about the nuances of relationship.[1] My work has been to try to get inside this word *relationship* and see what it is made up of. I tried to work with words that are available and to begin to ask about the dimensions of relatedness. Relationship is not unitary. We have very different kinds of relation-

Absence	Dimension	Excess
Falling	*Holding*	Suffocation
Aloneness, loss	*Attachment*	Fearful clinging
Inhibition, emotional deadening	*Passions*	Obsessive love
Annihilation, rejection	*Eye-to-eye validation*	Transparency
Disillusionment, purposelessness	*Idealization and identification*	Slavish devotion
Loneliness, dissonance	*Mutuality and resonance*	Merging
Alienation	*Embeddedness*	Overconformity
Indifference to others' needs	*Tending (care)*	Compulsive caregiving

FIGURE 2.1. Eight Dimensions of Relationship
SOURCE: © Sage Publications, 1997. This figure was previously published in Ruthellen Josselson, *The Space Between Us: Exploring the Dimensions of Human Relationships*. San Francisco: Jossey-Bass, 1992.

ships with different people. And even when people are in the same role relationship to us—such as a spouse or a child—how the relationship is emotionally constituted differs enormously from one to the other.

Many theorists have, of course, described and reflected on the nature and dynamics of human relationships. Yet although each has contributed a piece of the overall puzzle, many have then tried to derive all of human relationship from that single form of connection. After reviewing the literature and doing many interviews, I constructed a *relational space* that includes eight dimensions along which relationships might be located (see Figure 2.1). I will present a brief description of each dimension, as these will form the framework for our exploration of relationships among those who were raised communally.

The first four dimensions are primary in the sense that they are present from the beginning of life or shortly thereafter: holding, attachment, passions, and eye-to-eye validation. The second four dimensions require maturation and may not develop until late childhood. Idealization and identification (which is a single dimension) and embeddedness require a concept and experience of the self and the capacity to think about how one is positioned in regard to others. Mutuality and tenderness are also very much concerned with responsiveness to others and require development out of egocentrism and into a world of others.

The most basic of relational dimensions is that of *holding*, an aspect of relatedness much explored by Winnicott. The very earliest experience is that of feeling arms around one, being supported. With development, people who have been adequately held feel confident of survival, expect that basic needs will be met and that the world will not let them fall. Children who have been held well feel safe enough and protected enough to begin discovering aspects of themselves in the world. There is an experience of basic trust and support from the world, the core of an expectation that the world will not let one fall. We grow only within the context of adequate holding environments, which we may then take inside ourselves as a source of comfort and support. A great many people and institutions are potentially available for children, adolescents, and adults to use as holding environments as they grow. Schools and teams can hold; teachers, clergy, and therapists all hold. These people provide support—that is, hold, keep someone from falling. Friends may provide holding, but holders may also betray and disappoint. Often, the first heterosexual relationships in adolescence are primarily holding relationships, sexuality being relegated much to the background. Sometimes we find this pattern in marriage as well.

A bit later in earliest development, babies learn to discriminate their mothers from the other people around, making possible *attachment* to this one very particular other person. Bowlby has been the major theorist here. He considers the attachment system to be ethologically and biologically determined, necessary throughout life, and always distinguished from dependency. Attachment, unlike holding, requires that someone be in the world. One cannot be attached to someone who is not there. The propensity to attach to others structures some of the most fundamental processes throughout life, including the painful vulnerability to loss that is part of our human core. When we are attached, it is as though we are clinging to someone, holding on with our limbs, keeping close. Throughout life, we continue to form attachments (if we are fortunate), and these are often at the center of our existence.

Unlike the quiet security of attachment or the sense of solidity about being held, the passionate experience is noisy and insistent. The passions take center stage. The passions are intense aspects of experience that are charged, that claim our attention. In the realm of the passions, others are there to satisfy our drives and our quest for union. Much of psychoanalytic theory has articulated the vagaries of passionate connection as it wends through life. The pleasures of touch and erotic excitement, as well as the possibilities of uniting in boundaryless bliss, are powerful means of transcending space. In one form or another, people seek intense connection with others. Here the nature of the connection may be less important than its strength of emotional arousal. Some theorists, such as Fairbairn and Guntrip, have shown that we can feel intensely connected to each other through hurt, anxiety, or hate, as well as through pleasure.

The fourth dimension is *eye-to-eye validation*, in which we overcome space through the communication of eye contact, finding ourselves in the other's eyes, having a place in the other. In this aspect of relatedness, one finds oneself mirrored in another's eyes. The developmental history of eye-to-eye contact is learning about how others respond to us and how our responses to others affect them. How do you see me? we are asking. What do you think of me? Kohut has had a central role in helping us to recognize the centrality of mirroring in growth. Through eye-to-eye relating, we discover our meaning to others and what we can come to believe about ourselves. By being real to another, we become real to ourselves. But we can also be misapprehended, or we can see in the other's eyes the wish for us to be different than we are. Through eye-to-eye contact also comes vulnerability to the emergence of a "false self" (Winnicott, 1965), falseness residing in an identity that is not our own. Here we try to exist only for the approval of the other, finding ourself in the other's eyes and losing ourself in the process.

These first four dimensions are present in very young children and babies, but developmentally, we come to the fifth dimension of relatedness only after existing for a time in this world of others. Eventually, as children, we begin to notice that some people are bigger, stronger, and more able to do things than we are. Then we begin to relate to them through *idealization and identification*. We pattern ourselves using templates derived from others. The development of interests, values, and even careers wends through a narrative of identification, with friends and strangers as well as with parents and teachers. Identifications, then, are building blocks of identity. We pull ourselves along through life in an often-checkered fashion, based on our identifications with others. We also need people who embody ideals that we can internalize and reach toward. Without heroes, life loses its vitality (Kohut, 1977).

The sixth dimension of relatedness, *mutuality and resonance*, involves needs for sharing of experiences that neither shore up one's concept of self nor lead to growth-producing changes. As the person grows through childhood and the self matures and becomes more aware of others, the child will eventually discover the possibilities of engaging the self with others and will become able to experience companionship, which is a form of mutuality. In mutuality, we stand side by side with someone, moving in harmony, creating a bond that is the product of both people, an emergent "we" in the space between.

In this dimension are needs for companionship, walking side by side with someone, playing together, "hanging out" or "talking to," as my participants often describe this experience. This is an important dimension of human development and experience that I think is the least explored or understood. *Friend* is the name we give to someone with whom we experience mutuality and resonance. In friendship reside companionship and sharing, self-disclosure, and interpenetration of selves. Friendship may also involve loyalty, affection, competition, envy, and a host of other things. Friendship is what we have created mutually, the invisible bonds of the space between.

Miller, Jordan and others at the Stone Center have explicated the importance of the growth of the capacity for mutuality as it evolves in the therapeutic process (Jordan, 1986; Miller, 1988; Surrey, 1987). In their view, the experience of mutuality underlies zest for living. Emotional mutuality provides a necessary sense of aliveness that mitigates existential aloneness. It is this sense of "us"—a participation in the space between a you and a me—that connects us in a deeper and richer sense of our existence. And this, of all the dimensions, is the hardest to talk about, partly because it exists so completely between selves.

The seventh dimension of relatedness, *embeddedness*, involves belonging, finding, and taking a place with others. This is one of the central questions posed by adolescents. What shall I stand for? How will I fit in? Where might there be a place for me? Embeddedness, like holding and attachment, is silent rather than active and eventful. It is the framework that gives shape to selfhood, the context in which we define ourselves, the togetherness in which we are alone. The issues of embeddedness are the issues of the individual in group life. In defining the context of all relatedness, our embeddedness in a social context limits and gives meaning to all of our other relationships. Embeddedness is the soil in which other relatedness grows. Our connections to others always exist within a cultural set of meanings forming a web of interdependence, as well as a lexicon for interpretation of experience.

Being social creatures, we need to find a place within a social context, to join a culture, to entwine our individual experience with an ongoing human narrative. Learning language becomes our first act of embeddedness. How we speak, our form of communication, ever after denotes our connection to culture. We "speak" from our place within a society. To be embedded within a social network is to feel included, to share characteristics, to be the same as, to give up some individuality in the service of interconnection.

The eighth dimension of relatedness is *tending and care*. The experience of tending is one of offering to another what we experience to be good inside of us. We offer our emotional resources. We put aside our own needs and demands in the interest of another. We are, then, what we have to give. But care is not selfless—it does not obliterate the self. Instead it is a way of linking the self to the other.

Taking care can involve not only taking care of people but taking care of a relationship. Identity may reside in the effort to preserve and nurture relatedness. We have a rudimentary idea that the ability to give to others evolves naturally from having been given enough oneself. But we know little really about the origins of care or about its various forms of expression.

All of these modalities, then, are forms of reaching through the space that separates us, both physically and psychologically. Any given relationship may involve more than one of these dimensions, simultaneously or sequentially. How and toward whom love is expressed varies by culture. Yet there are certain fundamental human propensities for connection that find expression in some form universally. Social mores and traditions regulate the rituals and forms through which people are held or recognized or idealized, but the processes of these eight dimensions remain identifiable.

When we look at the phenomenology of personal experience, we find that the dimensions vary in their centrality in a given life. Although each of the dimensions is probably present to at least some extent in everyone's life, people often develop along particular relational pathways highlighting one or two relational themes in favor of others. Thus, some people tell life stories marked by needs for preserving attachment and caring for others. Other people narrate lives of trying to be "seen" by others as a certain kind of person—successful or desirable or intelligent. Others seek in their life projects to be like someone they admired, consecrating their life to realization of idealization.

These dimensions of relatedness unfold simultaneously and often independently, although they may interpenetrate. They are not, however, reducible one to another. Because human life is of a piece, the dimensions shade into one another; they do not stay separate and distinct, as well they should not. But each has its own coherent center, its own fundamental phenomenology.

NOTE

1. Some feminists have suggested that because language was devised by men, it takes little account of relational activity.

3 THE DIALOGUE BEGINS

Ruthellen: Over the years, people have tried to understand something about how the social organization of the kibbutz has affected relationships in adult life and how the kibbutz's style of child-rearing might affect later relationships. One question is how the social ecology of the kibbutz makes certain kinds of relationships possible and other kinds of relationships impossible, or makes them more likely or less likely. Another question is about the long-term effects on the development of relationships. One of the problems, as I see it, and as I think all of us see it, has been that the efforts to address these questions have, in large part, been global efforts that talk about whether people have more intimate relationships in the kibbutz, or whether people have bad relationships in the kibbutz—very vague, general kinds of terms.

One of the things that we've concluded, as we've been talking this year about our interviews and our work, is that people have a variety of experiences regarding relationships, so that in some ways, relationships might be better as a result of living or growing up communally, and in other ways, the relationships might be less desirable. The point of using this dimensional scheme is to try to talk about different ways in which people experience these relationships. What we are going to try to do is to put our heads together in terms of our different experiences with interviews and research to try to make some sense out of this. Can we as psychologists understand something about kibbutz members' experiences that will help us understand the larger developmental questions in general? Understanding not only the kibbutz, but also what the kibbutz experience tells us about relationships?

Here is a quotation from Martin Buber that I think raises some of these questions, and I wanted to read it as a way of initiating the discussion. It's from *The Knowledge of Man:*

> We may speak of social phenomena wherever the life of a number of men, living with one another, bound up together, brings in its train shared experiences and reactions. That to be thus bound up together means only that each individual existence is enclosed and contained in a group existence. It does not mean that between one member and another of the group there exists any kind of personal relation. They do feel that they belong together in a way which is, so to speak, fundamentally different from every possible "belonging together" with someone outside the group. And there do arise, especially in the life of smaller groups, contacts which frequently favor the growth of individual relations. But, on the other hand, frequently make it more difficult. In no case, however, does membership in a group necessarily involve an existential relation between one member and another....
>
> In general, it must be said that the leading elements in groups, especially in the later course of human history, have rather been inclined to suppress the personal relation in favor of the purely collective element. Where this latter element reigns alone, or is predominant, men feel themselves to be carried by the collectivity, which lifts them out of loneliness and fear of the world and lostness. When this happens—and for modern man, it is an essential happening—the life between person and person seems to retreat more and more before the advance of the collective. The collective aims at holding in check the inclination to personal life; it is as though those who are bound together in groups should in the main be concerned only with the work of the group and should turn to the personal partners, who are tolerated by the group, only in secondary meetings. (Buber, 1965, pp. 72-73)

Amia: This sounds like a statement, that is either-or, stating that there is limited energy, or limited resources for relationship, and it works like a conflict. . . . He was very famous as one of the ideologists of the kibbutz, and this passage sounds very familiar from the early kibbutz writings and their early approaches to forming the family and couple relationship, as we will see in some examples.

Ruthellen: I didn't realize that he may have been specifically addressing the kibbutz.

Amia: But what other collectivities are so strong that he could talk about modern man and collectivity? A monastery?

Ruth: Could it be any group, any kind of community?

Amia: Well, but concretely, speaking of the first half of the century, the beginning of the century, what did Buber see when he spoke about collectivity, other than the kibbutz—a synagogue, a temple?

Ruthellen: I think he may have meant a political group or any kind of tight group where the attachment to the group would be greater than the attachment to the individual, but I think the question that he raises here is the question that a lot of people who studied the kibbutz—Bettelheim, for example—have raised, namely, that somehow the massive pressure to join the collectivity interferes with personal relationships, and that is, in a sense, what a lot of the interviewees talk about.

Amia: It is also ideologically put that way. I can provide some quotations, and the kibbutz I researched is not the oldest one. When it started in the late 1920s, there were already kibbutzim about 20 years old. They were very strict, even prohibiting the couple relationship, or love relationship, in an exclusive manner, because they felt that it was against the community.

Ruth: We will have to discuss the impact of the collective. First, the ideology of the commune was to abolish private possessions and the family structure. Second, the fact that the commune was a very tight community affected personal intimacies. Thus, a single member of the commune would be asked to share a room with a couple, restricting intimacy. Another example of the community's intrusion was that its approval was necessary before a couple could have a child. Michal Palgi (1991) reports an interview with a woman who left the kibbutz in order to have a child because the collective was against motherhood at the time.

Amia: I think this was rare; I don't know many cases. But couples had to hide their love relationships. They never walked into the dining room or other places together. They really were ambivalent, because to be loyal to the whole group, you have to share all your feelings, and you cannot become exclusively related to one other.

Ruth: Amia, maybe you know more about this. I'm really curious about something. If they had to hide sexual expression, to avoid being seen together, sitting next to one another, or even touching, were they also encouraged to share sexual partners?

Amia: Muki Tzur (1988) writes about this part of the very, very early history of the communes, where sex was free, and people were encouraged to experiment with different couple relationships, but he says that it was very temporary, and while they tried to abolish the couples, there was no active process to introduce cross-relationships that would make them like a big family with different rules. This, he believes, is a result of the basic Jewish identity that all these people maintained. There were deep Jewish feelings about family life and about the sexual relationship as part of some organized institution.

Ruth: So if you had to place it on a continuum between puritanism and promiscuity. . . .

Amia: They were never promiscuous. Indeed, they were closer to puritanism.

Ruthellen: I find also, with my interviews, that there's relatively little sexual exploration or promiscuity among the people that I interviewed. . . . We have started out talking about the passions dimension, about intense couple relationships and the efforts to legislate them or to control them in the collective. It seems that that's one place where things didn't turn out the way they supposed. They hoped that they could break up the strong coupled-ness that people tended to form.

Ruth: It seems that contradictory ideologies coexisted in the commune. One was a puritanical code, and the other, free love. In Joshua Sobol's (1977) play, which is based on diaries from that period, this contradiction comes through. One of my speculations is that the founders were really mired in adolescent conflicts. They had left their homes in Europe and were searching for identity, alternating between Zionist, socialist, and some Freudian ideologies. This was a necessary developmental phase before they could settle down and start families. I wonder if there were differences between kibbutzim or between different phases of the group over time. I haven't thought about it until now, that the joiners might have belonged to an adolescent cohort, perhaps not in actual age but at least in terms of developmental phase.

Amia: Yes, it was true in terms of age, and they had no adults to imitate. It was a very unusual community of similar ages. If somebody was 25, he was considered old. But maybe we should go into this in the "passions" section when we reach it. I wanted to say something else by way of introduction. When I was re-reading my material for this meeting, and I looked through the different people who mentioned anything relevant to relationships, I came out with what you may say is a very self-evident conclusion: I almost never find a quotation relevant to a relationship in men's accounts of the kibbutz; it is always in the women's accounts. All my material (and you'd need several days to go through the different quotations) comes from female members—young, old, middle aged. The men speak about the security, about the wars, about creating the economy, the different ideological crises.

Ruth: Not even the family?

Amia: Never, never. Men from the second generation speak a little bit about early memories of the peer group in the common children's room; this is the only thing that I find. And it is such a prominent difference. You may say "well, what did you expect?" But when I did *Kibbutz Makom* in 1978, I was not aware of this. Later developments in psychology, theories such as Gilligan's (1982) and others, claim that relationships are a major trait or aspect of feminine life, and this kibbutz material has wonderful evidence for it.

Ruth: Men in your sample did not mention relationships at all? Not even mentors, or someone from work?

Amia: No. There is what Ruthellen calls an ideology, and this is where men come in, but even that is put in a more "rational" manner. It is phrased on an intellectual level, and the vast majority of discussion of any type of relationship comes from women's reports.

Ruth: Which generation is this?

Amia: All generations. I interviewed people in 1978, but at that time, I interviewed more than 120 people, and they were of all different generations, starting from age 16, up to the oldest member.

Hadas: Actually, I noticed that even though I asked my subjects explicitly about their relationships, and the whole interview was about relationships, the men spent a larger proportion of the interview talking about ideological issues than did the women. But there were a few of the men students, who were living outside the kibbutz, who seemed to have discovered relationships and started thinking about them and contemplating them for the first time in their lives.

Ruth: This is after they leave the kibbutz?

Hadas: Yes. It is perhaps the combination of being outside the kibbutz and in a student environment that seems to result in their being more sensitive in general to personal relationships. But basically, in our data as a whole, we found that men talk more about ideology than women do, much more.

Ruthellen: So we are talking here about the fact that we have to keep in mind this difference between the two sexes, that the male experience and the female experience might really be very different, which is certainly true in understanding the relationships in any society. That's not just true about the kibbutz. It's very clear, for example, that if we look at the developmental studies of men that have been published, relatedness is very much a subtheme, if it exists at all. And it's not clear whether it's because men don't experience it so much or whether they just don't talk about it.

Ruth: Several studies by Reis and associates (e.g., Wheeler, Reis, & Nezlek, 1983), studies of gender differences in patterns of intimacy and self-disclosure, show that intimacy is contextual for men; that is, once men find themselves in conversation with women, conversation that calls for intimate communication, they have no trouble being self-disclosing. Thus, we can rank the intimacy of dyads: at the top are woman-woman combinations, followed by woman-man, and, at the bottom, man-man. Another factor that may have been operating in the kibbutz is that there was no need to articulate intimacy or express emotions because these were taken for granted. The need for articulation may arise only in situations in which there is a threat of loss.

Another comment that I wanted to make relates to what Hadas said about interviewing in the context of the university and being more aware of relationships. I think this is an essential theme of the kibbutz for me: the way in which members of the kibbutz may be taking for granted their relationships in the kibbutz. They may only become aware of the nature of these relations once they are out of the kibbutz. This becomes more prominent when we talk about peers and the peer group. It seems that while you are there as a member, you are aware of certain things; once you leave it, then you become aware of things you took for granted. It is similar to the attachment experiences, which you, Ruthellen, mentioned in the introduction to your book (Josselson, 1992)—that it is in the separation or in the loss that you can learn about the meaning of the relationship. I think I'm going to keep that in mind and somehow use it in understanding when we talk about relationships in the kibbutz.

Ruthellen: So we have to recognize that someone who is still very much in the middle of a relationship may be experiencing a great deal that they're not talking about, because it feels so much like the air that they breathe.

Ruth: I agree. They may talk about what they lack or what they would like to have, but not about what they assume or take for granted or may not even be aware of. In order to find this, we have to read between the lines.

Ruthellen: I think that one of the things that is useful about us collaborating in this way is that, since we've used different methodologies, we can look at some of this. Amia's point is that if she asks people more generally about their kibbutz experience, she gets this interesting phenomenon where the men don't talk about their relatedness, and the women do. And Hadas and I have both addressed people's relationships directly. Hadas asked them about loneliness, and I asked them about relatedness, and you've also asked about these issues. . . .

Ruth: Yes, my questions are very direct, and I specifically ask about intimacy, friendship, love, and comradeship.

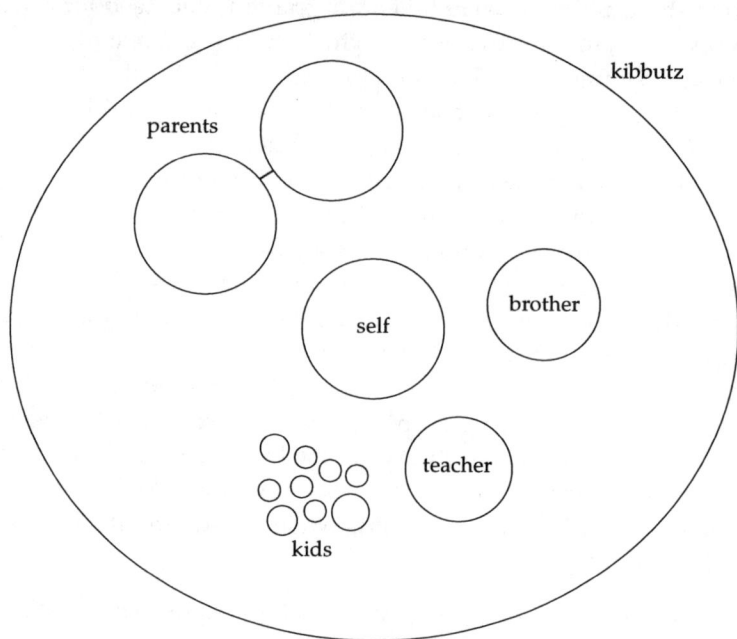

FIGURE 3.1. Shoshanna's Relational Map of Age 5

Ruthellen: Well, to get us started on the dimensions, here is an example of a person who grew up in a kibbutz. I wanted to show you how she represented her kibbutz experience (see Figure 3.1), because this relates to what you were talking about, Ruth, about the things you take for granted. The technique (for details, see Josselson, 1992) involves putting one's self in the center of a circle, and then around oneself are people who are important, and this larger circle is the kibbutz, and it's a very graphic representation of how the kibbutz feels, and it changes at different points in her life.

And then here, at 15 (see Figure 3.2), she says she's an observer of life, and at this point she's not sure she's still in the kibbutz, she's not feeling helped by it anymore. There's been a rupture, so it's now more in the distance than in the past.

And here, again, it's sort of in the background, as a place she could go back to if she wants to (see Figure 3.3). You notice at age 20 almost everybody disappears.

The Dialogue Begins

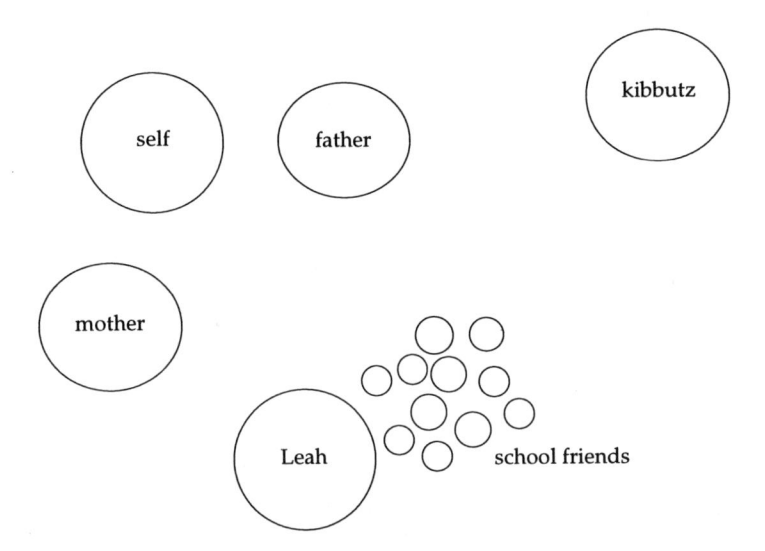

FIGURE 3.2. Shoshanna's Relational Map of Age 15

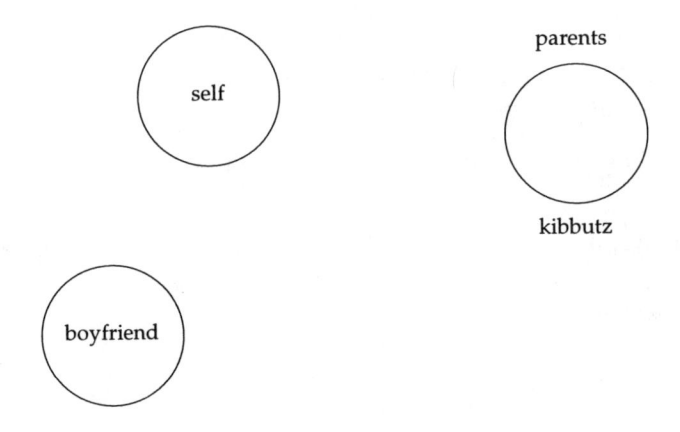

FIGURE 3.3. Shosanna's Relational Map of Age 20

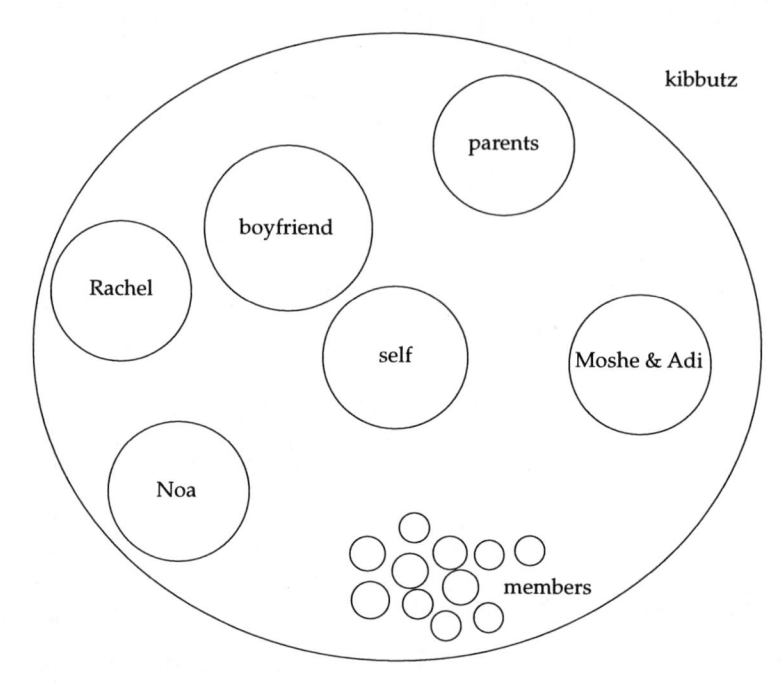

FIGURE 3.4. Shoshanna's Relational Map of Age 25

And then here, at age 25, she's back in the kibbutz again, and once again contained (see Figure 3.4). But it seems to me that this is a picture of a kind of a container.

Ruth: Yes, people are not always aware that they are living a certain way.

Ruthellen: That's right. In some way, it feels like a support, it's this "falling back on" sense that a number of people talk about. I would call it "holding."

4 HOLDING

Amia: Would you like to hear some quotations about holding?

Ruthellen: Sure.

Amia: The people speak about the kibbutz like a big home, and one of the nicest quotations comes from a third-generation kid. She was 20 when I interviewed her. Her grandfather is one of the founders of the kibbutz, both her parents live in the kibbutz, and she just finished the military service. She's in the stage of making a decision whether to remain in the kibbutz, or leave. It is 1978, it is not yet so popular to leave the kibbutz for long trips, or otherwise, and she's going to stay. So she says,

> I recall a realization I had while in the army. I was invited to the home of a girlfriend, and we took the bus together to her town, a suburb of Tel Aviv. As we got off the bus, I commented "How nice it is to have such a short drive to your home," and she answered, "This isn't my home yet, wait till we get there." And indeed we walked for another 40 minutes, her home was a tiny apartment in a big building, and only when she opened the locked door, was she "home."

> Suddenly I realized how different my situation is. I have a long bus ride to the kibbutz, but then, the moment I get off the bus at the main road and step onto the local road leading into the kibbutz, I'm home. The road, the trees, all the houses, all the paths are my home. I realized how extensive and solid my home is, which gives me a tremendous backing and profound sense of security. To this day, however, I've not decided whether or not I want this security, because my attempt to cope independently with life is still no less important to me. I've never tried to live on my own.

This is a metaphorical way of relating to holding. Several people talked about the kibbutz as a big home that they have. As I said, it is often brought up as a negative thing as well.

Ruthellen: That's the conflict people feel. They feel caught between how good it feels to feel bounded and contained in this way and also how frightening it might be to be restricted and unable to move on their own. I have a quotation that goes with that one, too, Amia. This is a man who is in his late 20s, and he's talking about his early experience with the kibbutz. He was born on the kibbutz and raised communally, and he talks about it in what I think is a lovely, concrete way. He says: "I felt very safe and very clear there. Everything was in its place, everybody was working in their place, and all the buildings were in their place, and I knew where everybody was. Everybody knew me."

Amia: Exactly.

Ruthellen: And then when he talked about going to school outside, he said that, by contrast, it was not so known and safe. So there was a feeling of going outside. . . .

Hadas: I have an example of holding in relation to the communal sleeping arrangement, which I found rather unusual:

> Sleeping with the other children during my childhood, with four children's beds around me, always gave me a lot of sense of security, and sleeping at my parents' always made me feel less physically secure—I can't really explain it.

Holding

Ruth: As a clinician, I can't help asking: Is the security that the person derives from the peer group and the environment a substitute for the security derived from a specific individual, such as a mother? Do the kibbutz members attach themselves to the trees and the big circle and experience being held because there is no exclusive person from whom they can derive this experience?

Ruthellen: Well, I still find, in terms of the people that I've interviewed, that the parents are still central, they still come out as the first people (this is retrospective data, looking back and representing how things were at age 5, age 10). At age 15, parents often are less important, but even later on, within the circle, the central figures are parents, those are the people they are touching. So it seems to be that both of those things are there. . . .

Amia: But the difference is that you have something above and beyond the parent, it's like a bigger network. I have another quotation that is not so physical, that is already more like social realization. This again, is from a younger woman—her age is 29—and she actually left the kibbutz, so I interviewed her about her past life. She says,

> The positive aspect of the kibbutz life, which I haven't found anywhere else, is the idea and practice of reciprocal help. This is first and foremost in my mind, it is not just the mere fact that all your needs are provided for, whether you are sick, old, or whatever, it is the true concern for the well-being of every individual member by the group.

This is the collective that Buber is talking about. She goes on,

> There is a deep understanding, a commitment, in a sense, and it touches me deeply. Take, for example, the recent trip to Sinai, which was organized for the elderly of the kibbutz: Every detail was thoroughly planned, and not by their children. When I heard about the deep concern of the youngsters, who helped the old ladies in walking, climbing, and in so many other ways, I thought that there is no urban society that could compete in this area with the tradition of our kibbutz.

Ruth: We see this in studies of children: Kibbutz children behave more cooperatively and share more than others (Shapira, 1976). However, in several of my own studies comparing city and kibbutz children, kibbutz children were less likely to view members of the peer group as helpful (Sharabany, 1982). Moreover, when asked about their best friends, kibbutz youngsters reported fewer requests and fewer offers of help than their urban cohorts (Sharabany, 1974). It appears that while helpfulness is the norm in kibbutz society, one's personal experience of help is a different matter.

Amia: But the community is built to answer the need. Of course, people have to know who is in need, but the holding is to take the elderly and to think ahead of time that they will need somebody to help them climb or to build rooms that will be central so that the elderly will have easier access to the dining room and to the culture hall and so on. This is again partly physical, but a lot of it is social concern, which I think is holding, and it provides the holding function for different age groups, in a manner that is appropriate to the age group.

Hadas: In terms of the dimensions, one needs to ask what is the meaning of this big circle? How is holding by the big environment different from holding within a one-to-one mother-child context, and does it have negative sides as well as positive sides? Because it might be easier to help an older woman from the kibbutz to walk than to help your own grandmother.

Ruth: I think that your data may represent individual differences. While some people may report experiencing and appreciating help on the personal level, when you look at kibbutz members as a group, the mean level of help reported is lower.

Amia: But this is quite common, this realization of holding in a positive manner. In the late 1970s, when I did *Kibbutz Makom*, people were not so critical of the kibbutz as they were 10 years later, when Hadas and I were collecting our interview material. Here is another quotation about the same issue, and I eliminated a lot of the repetitions. When a repetition remains, it usually means that this occurred many, many times. This is a woman who is 54 (again a woman, you see). She is not married, and she talks about being single. And she says,

Holding

> To be single is not great anywhere, but I think it's easier in the kibbutz. I don't have to worry about walking alone outside here, whatever the hour at night, whereas in the city, it is completely different. I don't mind going alone to parties or other events in the kibbutz because everybody is my friend. Growing old alone here is much less threatening. I know that no matter what happens to me, sickness, accident, I'll be completely taken care of by the kibbutz....

And she compares it to the town, and I think these are holding experiences that are very profound.

Hadas: In the age group that I interviewed, ages 20 to 30, everybody did emphasize that they felt they could always return to the kibbutz, that they would always be taken care of. These people stressed that what is good about the kibbutz is the peacefulness and nature, and knowing that if something happens there is always someone who is going to take care of them. But this very fact creates a dilemma. This quotation comes from a woman and she lives in the kibbutz, but a lot of people who left the kibbutz said this too:

> The thing is, is it in your experience something good, that there is always someone to take care of you, or do you reject it, and say "no, I have to do it on my own? I know I can always return to the kibbutz, but that would be a total defeat."

But still, there is a very strong sense that there would always be someone there, and also, if your parents died, God forbid, or something, there is always this very strong thing that is always going to be there. As some of the interviewees put it, "even if all the youngsters are going to leave the kibbutz, the kibbutz is still going to be there."

Amia: However, some people also looked at this negatively, even then. There is a woman of 29 who says,

> You see, a big kibbutz like Makom can provide many social and vocational opportunities for its members, if they find their place within the society. But if they don't, it can be like a prison, being

in constant contact with individuals you don't really care about, or with people with whom you haven't even chosen to be. I prefer to be alone, rather than in continuous contact with these people who aren't really my friends.

That's the other side of the holding. I have several of these quotations, and Hadas has many.

Hadas: But do you think it's the opposite side of holding, that is, restricting (i.e., excess of holding), or is it the opposite side of validation?

Ruthellen: What I think this person is talking about is the experience of being held in the community, where the sense of who she is, the way in which she's recognized, is very painful. And so you get caught with your security being in a place where the way you're seen by others is not how you wish to be seen. And I think that that's what the sense of the prison is. She's not talking so much about the fact that she can't get out, but that she has to live in this place, with people who don't look at her in a way that she wishes to be looked at, or that she didn't choose. Although I find enormous variation in the experiences of people who have been raised on the kibbutzim, the thing that I find most common to them is the sense of basic security. There is the feeling that there is something they can fall back on, whether they're still in the kibbutz or not. They have this sense that they are supported, that they are held from underneath, somehow, by this early experience.

Hadas: I have an example of a bad experience in the communal sleeping arrangement, which represents the opposite of what I read to you at the beginning, and you can't really say that either of them is unusual.

> I had a very, very rough childhood, in the communal sleeping arrangement, stories that you wouldn't believe about the "metaplot." They abused us physically, they made us eat terrible things ... very bad memories from 5 to 11. Maybe the metapelet was a Holocaust survivor. . . .

He says that his parents didn't interfere because they were afraid they would make things even worse. I took that as an example of when you don't have validation or eye-to-eye from your parents. However, he continues to say,

For me, the communal sleeping arrangement had connection to loneliness, because it's a feeling of being left, to always be left behind, and you want to sleep and other kids are making noise and you feel helpless. And on our kibbutz, it was very unusual to go sleep at your parents' house, it was something you wouldn't think of.

It's a Shomer HaTsair kibbutz, which is more strict in its ideological attitudes.

Ruth: I'm going to play the devil's advocate and question the idea of being able to fall back on the kibbutz. It reminds me of an interview in Lillian Rubin's (1985) book, *Just Friends*. The man says, "Yes, I have a buddy. He's very important to me, and I can always turn to him." When she asked when he had last seen this buddy, it turned out that their last meeting was 10 years earlier. When she asked where this buddy lived, the man said, "Well, I could find his address if I needed it."

I can think of situations in which the kibbutz does not extend help. In the past, children who left the kibbutz were disowned, not only by the group but also by their own parents. Now, children who leave for city life are not entitled to any financial support from the kibbutz, and their parents are often unable to help them. It is also possible that kibbutz members idealize the potential for help but don't risk testing it. Mary Main, in her adult attachment work, talks about idealization, and her definition of an idealization has opened my eyes (Main & Goldwyn, 1990). It's not just saying something is good, but an inability to find concrete examples of experience that support the idealized memory. So I would ask your subjects, When was the last time you requested help? What kind of help? What do you remember about being helped? And what was the actual outcome?

Amia: In the late 1970s, for example, there was a young family that I interviewed here, who left the kibbutz for a while. The husband was trying to make it financially as a bus driver, and in a couple of years, they got into a terrible financial squeeze and they couldn't pay for their apartment. Then the Yom Kippur War (1973) broke out, and he was on duty for months. She was pregnant, so she returned back home, first of all, to deliver the baby at the kibbutz with her mother's family. And then, when her husband was released from the military service (at that time, people were mobilized for 6 months or so, since it was an emergency), and he came back, they were evicted from their apartment near Tel Aviv because they didn't pay the rent. And she was with the baby.

Without any ideological conviction, actually acting against what were their plans for their life, they decided to stay in the kibbutz, to recuperate, and to find enough courage to try to make another attempt to leave. But they never went out. And she says that later she had another baby and her husband received some kind of a job in the kibbutz, and they felt that this was their place. I find this a good story of really going back and falling back on your parents and on the general community.

The community here was supportive, to the extent that they allowed this man to develop some of his hobbies, which helped him satisfy his needs, which were very individual. He was a scuba diver, so they allowed him to go to Eilat and they gave him the equipment, and they really tried to make life more bearable for him in the kibbutz. And the family never left. With the years, since I've been visiting, they are one of the families with which I really became close friends. I know that they made a wonderful adjustment. The woman was once the secretary of the kibbutz, and he became kind of a youth leader. He encouraged children to do horseback riding, and scuba diving. The return to the kibbutz was a solution to a family crisis, and here the kibbutz is clearly a holding environment for them.

Hadas: And why did they leave in the first place?

Amia: She left because of a bad relationship with her mother, exactly from a separation-individuation point of view. Her mother was a very important figure in the kibbutz. She left because she felt she could never live up to her parents' expectations. It is the story of the leader's children, who really were under terrible pressure to superachieve, to surpass what their parents did, and to be always good. I have a quotation about it, when she says,

> The constant pressure to be OK, to fulfill the expectations of the society, and to be always under supervision and control, and to be judged for every little thing, especially in work, but also in your private life, everybody knows what you do or don't do, and this made my life very difficult.

That is the stage before she left.

Ruthellen: That moves into the validation dimension, which is a different matter. It's interesting that you, Ruth, brought up that example from Lillian Rubin, because I was very struck by that, too, and I had quite a different understanding of it. I thought she missed something there. She seemed very quick to label this—you know, this is a man, this is how men have friendships, his best friend is someone whom he hasn't seen in 10 years, and he doesn't even know where he lives, and that's a man's best friend.

But it seems to me that there is something about the internalization of a relationship that becomes important for how one builds one's life and stabilizes oneself. So the fact that this person could feel as though he has a best friend, even though it's someone he hasn't been in contact with, may to him be as meaningful as the women whose best friend lives across the street, and she sees her every day. That woman may need to have this contact on a daily basis in order to experience herself as really connected to somebody. However, this guy feels that as long as he knows that somewhere in the world is someone he could call up if he really touches bottom, then that's enough for him.

So whether or not people use that contact may be different from whether they feel like they have it. I think that this has been true in the kibbutz sample, that a number of people have talked about the experience of disillusionment, which has to do with idealization, in the sense that "I always believed that was there for me, and then when I tested it, and I asked for something from the kibbutz, then they didn't come through, and I had to rethink my whole sense of what reality was."

The other point that I wanted to make, which I think is important in getting into this question about separation-individuation in the kibbutz, is that the more secure people feel in terms of having a holding environment, the more they may feel free to experiment and reject it. And that goes back to the sense of taking for granted. It may be that people who are most outspoken about criticizing the kibbutz, trying this and that in leaving it, are the people who most benefited from this early sense that there was something they really could rely on. And some of the interviewees do say that they feel they're free to go out in the larger world, because they can always go back if they should feel the need.

Ruth: I agree with your point, which illuminates the complexity and paradox of the psychological processes. Your emphasis on internalization is similar to the Eriksonian notion of developing a sense of basic trust, which is a general feeling, a core feeling. Maybe this general trust enables exploring, moving away, criticizing, and so on. However, it is possible that when people find a discrepancy between their reported general feeling of friendship, trust, and so on and their ability to substantiate this claim by giving examples to back it, then we are observing a different, defensive process.

Amia: These are perhaps different attitudes toward social reality. We can agree that the social reality of the kibbutz is peculiar and has its own specific characteristics, which are not frequently encountered in other types of communities. This general collectivity has created in people quite a profound sense of being held by much more than the nuclear family, or the people with whom they have had personal relationship. We have a sense of a holding environment, which is larger and based not only on people but on structure, on ideas, and so on. People may rebel against it, it may also have negative aspects, but it is there, as can be shown by many demonstrations.

Hadas: The negative aspect is feeling too tightly held, because it's like so many hands are holding you, you want to brush them off.

Ruth: Yes, and there is another problematic effect. The holding by the kibbutz as a community, in general, as a circumscribed geographic area, like a big home, is the positive outcome. However, other people may feel that everyone is meddling or interfering, and there is no one specific person who would be their secure base.

Hadas: What do you mean by "no one specific"?

Amia: The kibbutz doesn't answer your needs.

Ruth: The kibbutz doesn't see you. You don't have a particular person. Maybe I am now talking about attachment. The kibbutz offers, perhaps, a diffuse sort of holding.

Hadas: I'd like to read to you just one example that demonstrates the sense of loving the kibbutz, but also feeling too tightly held:

> To grow up in the kibbutz means, on the one hand, to love it very much and to feel deeply attached to it and, on the other hand, to always want to get away from it, escape from these parents. You

have many parents who are always wrapping, covering you. Instead of a pair of parents, you have many parents who want you to stay home. And like every normal city youngster who wants to leave his/her parents, we do too. And I'm like that, the kibbutz is like a home for me. The people on the kibbutz, on the one hand, are very close to me; on the other hand, they suffocate me.

Ruthellen: That's exactly the negative side, the feeling that you can't breathe because it's too much.

Amia: Shall we go on to attachment?

5 ATTACHMENT

Ruthellen: In early life, I think it's hard to discriminate between holding and attachment. For the very small child, these are fused, but as development proceeds, they become quite different, and one can feel attached to people one isn't held by, and held by people one isn't attached to. What I've learned about people raised communally on the kibbutz is that beyond their experience of the kibbutz as a general holding environment, they seem to feel very clear about whom they belong to, who their parents are, who are the people to whom they are primarily attached. I was very surprised about this. Although I don't have a very large sample, I don't see any difference, in the sense of belonging and primary attachment, between those who were raised in the kibbutzim and those who were raised in the city.

Amia: I think this is a basic myth about the kibbutz family, which was presented by Spiro (1958) and by Bettelheim (1969), and by the early research, as breaking the parent-child intimacy and relationship. We all agree by now that it is not a true picture, that in spite of the fact that children didn't sleep at home, with all the details that we will discuss in a moment, children were very much attached to their own biological parents, and they distinguished between them and others. Many things were said about the kibbutz in this respect which are simply untrue.

Ruth: It's not only attachment that matters but also the kind of attachment. I'm coming from the perspective of attachment theory, developed by Bowlby (1969/1982), Mary Ainsworth et al. (1978), and Mary Main. Ainsworth posits that everyone is attached but that there are three major patterns of attachment: secure, avoidant, and ambivalent. Avi Sagi and his associates at Haifa University found a greater incidence of the ambivalent attachment pattern among kibbutz children than among city children (a recent review of the work is found in Aviezer, Van Ijzendoorn, Sagi, & Schuengel, 1994). It seems to me that this finding sheds light on the situation in the kibbutz: A larger percentage of kibbutz children exhibit insecurity in their attachment to mothers and caretakers. Among the kibbutz-born, communally raised babies, Sagi and associates found a greater percentage of what is called the C type, those who are attached in an ambivalent way (angry and resentful). In contrast, a greater percentage of the secure type were infants of women who came to the kibbutz from England or other Anglo-Saxon countries. Although this is a very narrow definition of *secure attachment* that comes from a particular paradigm of research, it sheds an interesting light. Based on episodes of separation and the reaction to them, a difference was found between kibbutz-raised and city-raised children: A higher rate of kibbutz-raised children were insecure, a finding similar to what Bettelheim talked about.

Amia: How was it measured?

Ruth: The researchers used Ainsworth's "strange situation"; they observed the child interacting with and separating from father, mother, and caretaker separately.

Ruthellen: It's very hard to interpret the "strange situation" data in the context of the kibbutz, because these are children who, from the very beginning, are always being left with other people. What the strange situation does is measure the response of the child to being left with other people, so you have a built-in confounding here, which is very hard to straighten out, and it's very hard for me to know what to make of that data from the kibbutz. Although I have been much influenced by Bowlby's attachment theory, I'm also very interested in the phenomenon of attachment through life.

I can't think in terms of the strange situation in adulthood, but I can think in terms of people's early sense of "belonging to," which I think is a phenomenological aspect of attachment, once it can be cognitively represented. The sense that "these are somehow the people that I belong to, who are my people, who are somehow the people who keep me from aloneness." Not so much providing security, which for me is holding, but keeping me from aloneness. These are the people whom I will go through life with, who will somehow have to be there for me, not to take care of me, or to do things for me, or maybe even to protect me, except in the sense of feeling protected because I am not alone. Not because you actually pull me away from the fire because it is going to burn me, but because here we are alone at night and it's scary, and if you're there with me, I don't feel as afraid as if I were alone in the house at night and I heard the noises.

Rather than the strange situation, I am interested in looking at people's representation of their parents throughout the life cycle, in terms of their sense of connection to them. What I find is that those people who are raised in the kibbutz maintain contact with their parents. They stay connected to them; they have a strong sense of this more global kind of attachment. They go to visit them, they stay concerned about their welfare, they have a feeling that this is part of their family, and because they're in the family, they have to somehow go through life together. I don't see any differences between those who were raised communally in the kibbutzim and those who were raised in the city on that particular domain. Some people, obviously, have closer and more important sorts of attachments to parents than others, but that's true equally, so far as I can tell.

Amia: I would like to talk about a feature of the kibbutz family that is very Israeli and very Jewish, the thing you read and hear about the family that is multigenerational. Even though you are already having your own children, you maintain close relationships with your older parents and other members of the extended family. I think that, in this sense, the kibbutz is very Jewish, in maintaining the importance of the three generational family. Kibbutz members use the concept of the *hamula* (clan), which is really a big family. It has become a political power in the community, and the larger it is, the more powerful it is in the kibbutz society. I guess that this is not so much the kibbutz itself, but the general Israeli atmosphere. Different sociologists studying the family in Israeli society, for example, Peres and Katz (1980), call Israel a very "familistic" society, and the kibbutz today is one of the strongholds of this general family focus.

Ruthellen: It's interesting to me that this is in the context of a deliberate effort to work against familization. The initial ideology in the kibbutz was to break all that up. Therefore, they called the children "the children of the kibbutz" and "the son or daughter of the kibbutz," and people were not supposed to refer to their parents as "my mother" or "my father" but to call them by their first names. There really wasn't supposed to be this exclusive quality about it at all. It seems as though that was not something that they were successful doing, that the ideology really didn't prevail. Even for the people that I interviewed at a Shomer HaTsair kibbutz, which was the most radical, exclusivity still existed underground. People still knew whom they belonged to.

The other thing that I find interesting here is that, in the Rabin and Best-Hallahmi (1982) study, they found differences in attachment between those who were raised on the kibbutz and those raised on the moshav. They reported a difference in attachment—not Bowlby attachment but as they defined it—which had to do, I think, with maintaining contact and feeling connected in an ongoing way. Rabin, Best-Hallahmi and their associates found that those raised in the kibbutzim were less attached than those not raised there. But then they say, in one little offhand line, that this was only true for men. There was no difference in terms of the women maintaining contact and maintaining attachment. Only the men seemed to be less attached.

Amia: Regarding the historical background that you just mentioned, the effort to dismantle the family unit was a very short phase. Very soon they were willing to allow the normal flow of relationship between mother and children to go on somehow. In the material that I collected, women, especially older women, were critical of the kind of motherhood they provided to their children, especially in contrast to the kind of motherhood that they can see their daughters providing now to their grandchildren. There is such a difference in what is allowed between a mother and her infant in the kibbutz today as opposed to 50 years ago.

This was the most painful part of the accounts I received, and many of the elderly women were really weeping while telling me about how they agreed willingly to take upon themselves the very strict rules and regulations about child care. For instance, if a child would cry, you were never allowed to go to the crib and pick it up, because it was under the supervision of the metapelet. Mothers were told that the babies would be fed when the time to feed comes, and this should "strengthen" them, build their character, not giving in to these needs of the screaming babies. One of the mothers, who was really a tough lady, became so soft for a moment when talking about this. She said,

> We didn't have strollers at that time. The idea of taking the child for a walk was out of the question. My baby was crying every evening at 6 o'clock, and we know this is a time when many infants become quite agitated, and I would come, in a masochistic way, to the children's home and stand outside and hear my baby screaming, and cry, and know that I'm not allowed to interfere. I would go back and feel kind of purified because I was doing the right thing to create the next generation of babies that would be healthy and strong and real Israelis, and not *Galut* type, not diaspora type.

Ruth: Was she a first-generation kibbutz member?

Amia: She was a founder. She herself comes from such a warm family, from eastern Europe. She tells such warm stories about her father and mother and their lovely relationship, and all the siblings, and the Shabbat. Again, there is the contrast between the family that she comes from and the willful attempt to break the pattern and to create a different thing, and now in retrospect, she is saying that it was all a mistake. By the way, now as an elderly widow, she tries to re-create the warmth of her family of origin in her present three-generation kibbutz family. This comes up in other stories, too. I want to read a part from another woman, who speaks about exactly the same experience:

> Makom had a rule, that children were not allowed into the dining room. They ate their dinner at the children's home, before they were brought to their parents' home, and later at night, before we put them to sleep, we would give them a snack in the apartment. The usual practice was that one of the parents stayed home with the children, while the other went for his meal, and then they switched.

But this woman, Na'ama, was alone. Her husband was on a mission in Europe, helping Jews out of the concentration camps. She was alone with two young kids, and she says,

> First, I used to put the baby to sleep, since her bedtime was still very early. Then I would leave my elder one, who was 3 when Oded left, alone in my room, to wait until I had returned from dinner. There was no way to eat in the room then—there was not even an electric kettle to boil water in. Who imagined that someday we would be cooking whole meals in the room? So my daughter used to stay alone in the room every evening when I went to dinner, and she is such a quiet, obedient girl, never protested or said a word.

Na'ama is crying, telling me this.

> I cannot forgive myself. Only years later did I find out how frightened this little girl was, how she lay in my bed trembling, afraid of snakes, afraid of all sorts of things, of the darkness, watching the door, watching for the moment I'd come back again. To this very day, it hurts me terribly. Why did we not understand then, how is it possible that I couldn't see what I was doing to my daughter? There was no one that gave it any consideration.

Again and again, she's blaming herself:

> All these rules and regulations were very strict then, even cruel, one might say. Some of them were the result of our difficult conditions, but others we accepted as principles of our volition. Maybe that's why it didn't seem difficult at the time, because we were living with our own personal choices. We were not bitter people, we knew fun and joy, pleasure and humor, we were in general happy people. What we lacked, perhaps, was the foresight, the necessary vision to direct ourselves.

They really did not want to imitate the way their parents brought them up. There were no other models, there were no people older than them in the community, people to consult with.

Ruthellen: Did you interview the daughter? Did she remember this experience?

Amia: Yes. The daughter, who is called Elisheva in the book, is among the women who were 40 when I interviewed them, who hated the common sleeping arrangement. Most of the women who talk about the common sleeping arrangement had a lot of criticisms, feelings ranging from hate to indifference. Most of the men, however, were terribly happy. They said it was an ongoing camp experience, and they enjoyed it. It was an ongoing party for the boys, whereas for the girls, it was very difficult.

Hadas: It is interesting that it seems you have to have the experience of motherhood to appreciate these issues. In our data, we found that a lot of the people in the sample of young adults—who weren't married and weren't really thinking of children yet—a lot of them said that they liked the communal sleeping arrangement, that it was fun, and so on, but that they wouldn't want it for their children. So there is the issue of this discrepancy: If they think it is so great, then why don't they want it for their children? Even the men said that maybe for their own children, they would choose otherwise. But you have to take the context into consideration as well, since now most kibbutzim have moved to the family sleeping arrangement.

Amia: Yes, my interviews refer to a time when my particular kibbutz was still very strict on the communal sleeping arrangement. But gradually it became less strict in the sense that children who had nightmares, and who had fears during the night, were allowed to sleep at home. And, of course, the mother was encouraged to take more natural care of the infant. At the time of the interviews in the late 1970s, mothers were breast-feeding all day. They could pick up their children, they could take them in the stroller, there was nothing against it anymore. But at this early time, when a child was sick, it was quarantined, sometimes for 2 weeks or 4 weeks, so that infections wouldn't spread, and the mother was not allowed to get near it, only the professionals. We all know that today hospital practices have changed tremendously, and parents are actually "hospitalized" together with their children.

Ruth: This change parallels a general change in the West and reflects a change in the Zeitgeist. In the fifties, the emphasis was on scheduling and hygiene. Maybe it reflects a difference in generations. I like to think of it as a pendulum-type situation. After one generation limited the maternal role, the next sought to enhance it. If, in the past, motherhood was lacking, in the present, it is characterized by abundance. My prediction is that the next generation will place the emphasis on careers and self-realization.

Ruthellen: We were talking about the ways in which kibbutz rules may have interfered with natural processes of attachment between mothers and children. I wonder what your sense has been about how attachment plays out with people in the kibbutz later in life. What happened in adult life to these people you studied?

Ruth: Rephrasing the question, we could ask whether multiple parenting can serve as a buffer against the effects of parental pathology. Nathan, Frenkel, and Kugelmass (1993) conducted a longitudinal study comparing high-risk kibbutz and city children with schizophrenic parents. They found no buffer effect in the kibbutz children. Shlomo Breznitz's (1985) interpretation is that whereas an emotionally handicapped city mother has numerous interactions with her children, many of which are connected with mundane chores, the kibbutz mother's interactions are centered around the love hour. If she is not up to the task emotionally, there is little else she can give her children.

Amia: Stigma is also important here. The children who grow up in the kibbutz are stigmatized if something is wrong with their family. It is something that you cannot run away from, and there is an expectation from the community that something is wrong with you too.

Ruthellen: I wonder if these are people whose parents were identified as psychotic and very, very deviant? The people I found were probably children of depressed mothers, who maybe were not so disturbed. I had a couple of subjects who had mothers who were Holocaust survivors and very depressed, and the mothers didn't have much available for nurturance. And the subjects both described how they were able to find somebody else, either a metapelet or just some other person who really could care for them. And as adults looking back, they would say "and I would go to that person if my mother was very depressed or she was sleeping or she couldn't be with me, then I could just to go the person next door" or "I felt that my metapelet really loved me and was somebody who I was attached to."

Ruth: This is very interesting. It probably depends on the pathology. There is a developmental study (Sameroff, Seifer, & Zax, 1982) which shows that for urban children, depressed mothers are more dysfunctional than schizophrenic ones.

Hadas: I have the very same subject saying both things, both that it's a buffering thing, that what saved him was being brought up on the kibbutz, but on the other hand saying,

> You know, I come from a very problematic family, and it affects how I'm looked upon. I'm always fighting with my label in the kibbutz, which is tied to my family background. I was a very problematic child and my family is problematic, and it's a label that was stuck to you.

The first time he felt free of that label was when he went abroad. It was the first time that he felt free of this image of his family. I think he had a brother who was severely mentally ill on the kibbutz.

Ruthellen: That has to do with the validation dimension. But I want to say one more thing about attachment, and you may wish to comment on this, too. I want to share the fact that so few people mentioned the metapelet as someone whom they had been attached to, or whom they remember strongly. I don't have the exact figures, but I think probably about one in five of the people that I interviewed put their metapelet on the chart. I was talking to Ofra Mayseless about that, and she suggested that perhaps the feelings about the metapelet just get fused back into the family, and that people don't remember the metapelet and the good caring specifically. That idea reminded me of one of our earlier discussions, in which we talked about our own experiences with our children who had caregivers when they were little. We talked about how we knew that they had intense and close relationships with their caregivers, but then the relationship just faded. They just didn't remember.

Ruth: And how did you understand it in terms of your own children?

Ruthellen: Well, it's hard to understand. Something about the sense of belonging. When the child can conceptualize that "this is the person I belong to," that relationship then becomes terribly important. If there isn't the feeling that there is going to be continuity, that this person will be with me through my life, then the quality of attachment is different—and evanescent.

Amia: It is kind of like a delegation. You delegate your feelings to this metapelet who takes care of your child, and the child understands: You are there in the morning, when he or she wakes up, and then you go for a couple of hours, or even for the whole day, but you're coming back, and you're the constant, and the other ones are delegated. If she's good, it reflects on you as a mother, that you are creating a good replacement, and that's it, but she remains a replacement.

Ruthellen: It becomes a holding environment.

Ruth: Maybe very few kibbutzniks mention the caretaker as someone they were attached to or remember because the experience is attributed to or integrated with the mother. While outsiders assume that kibbutz children have a single, constant caretaker, the truth is that this role is fulfilled by several different women. So very often, I think, we outsiders looking at the kibbutz, we call her "the" metapelet, but there isn't such a person. In the best case, a child may have the same metapelet for 2 years in a row.

Ruthellen: Some people talk about longer relationships, but in general, I think that's true. The paradox is that people often remain unattached to people who were consistently present and yet form strong attachments to people who were rarely present. In many cases, people will talk about attachment, for example, to fathers whom they rarely saw. Many of my interviewees talk about rarely seeing their fathers, especially those who were children of people who were very active in the kibbutz. The kibbutz makes so many demands on people that my interviewees would say, "for most of my childhood, my father wasn't around. I saw him only occasionally." And yet, there was this very strong sense that they belong to that father, that this was their father, and on the validation dimension, who their father was has very special meaning.

Hadas: I feel a sense that kibbutz men aren't as involved with children as the women are, that they have more important things to attend to, that they're always doing other things. Maybe it's less difficult for the kibbutz children, because they aren't the only ones whose parents aren't home. Everybody is that way.

Ruthellen: That's a very important point, which I think we can't say enough, that people interpret their experience based on what they see around them. That is always what we run into in this kind of research: There's the fact of the experience and there's the interpretation of the experience. And reinterpretations all through life, always based on the context. So I think your point is a wonderful one: that in the kibbutz, everyone sees how it is for everybody else, more so than in city life, I think, where you can have more fantasies about what's going on behind the closed doors. I think that people have more of a sense that their situation probably isn't very different from other people's, that nobody's father is around, and that everybody's mother is pressured during the 2-hour period.

Ruth: It is analogous to never being able to see families other than your own. Sullivan (1953) considers preadolescence the phase during which children have a chance to compare what goes on in their family (which was taken as the only model) with life in families of friends. In so doing, children give up the illusion that the whole world is the same. According to Sullivan, this process is very important to mental health, because it provides alternatives to pathological situations.

Hadas: Often, kibbutzniks get more attached to their parents in late adolescence. One person I interviewed said that the change was in the army, which is consistent with Amia's data (Lieblich, 1989). He first felt more of a bond with his parents during his army service, when he was away, and his parents were caring for him and worried about him. From the young adults, what you hear is, "Now I want to build more of a relationship with my parents. Now that I'm outside the kibbutz, I feel much more involved in my family." You don't hear that said with the same intensity by young adults in the city.

Ruthellen: But this might be—back to Ruth's point about taking for granted—that when living with their parents, they couldn't see or experience what was going on, and only when they got away could they see what was happening.

Ruth: The kibbutz child-rearing ideology did not attach significance to continuity. When children reached the age of 3, they left the children's house, the toys, and the caretaker. When I asked a kibbutznik about this, he replied, "But of course, we didn't need the baby stuff anymore. We were kindergarten children."

Amia: According to Bettelheim (1969), the continuous part is the peers, and I think that talking about attachment in the kibbutz, one of the things we should discuss is attachment to peers. It is very deep and primitive and primary. Remember what Hadas read us before, the four beds in the room and the children. Although they fight, and although they may hate each other, and so on, they create an essential attachment that replaces the nighttime figures of the parents, and this is a constant. The peers go with you from home to home. They are much more constant than the metapelet.

Ruthellen: For some, it's a holding sense, it's a sense of "this is the group." But it's very rare, at least in my data, for the connection to be an attachment relationship, a feeling that this is someone who I feel continuous with, who is there for me, who makes me feel not alone. In order to feel not alone, one has to have the specificity, a particular person who is physically there, which is different than holding, because you can be held by a nonspecific person who is not physically there. There's an analogy here to people's attachments to their analysts and therapists. Sometimes it can be a specific attachment, but it may instead be an attachment to therapy, especially if people had several therapists. One can be held by the idea that there is help available if one gets in trouble. People do sometimes internalize therapy as an institution, rather than a specific person. For what I think of as "real" attachment, you have to have the sense of a person there who will be with you, who makes you feel not alone, a person whom you can count on to be responsive. The kibbutz-raised people I spoke to don't really talk about peers in that way. Occasionally, a subject will say "I had a specific friend and we were a pair, and I always knew that he was there for me." But for most people, it's much more just the sense of being part of this group in an embedded sense, without the feeling that there was an individual who was there who could be counted on to be responsive. Actually, I hear more from nonkibbutz people about specific friends who serve as attachment figures. I think I only have one kibbutz-raised subject who had a lifelong friend.

Ruth: When kibbutzniks describe friends, they describe them as less intimate than city children describe their friends. This is in agreement with Ruthellen's impressions. In my research on attachment to peers as a group, I also did not find the positive attachment Ruthellen refers to

(Sharabany, 1982; Sharabany & Rosenthal, 1984). Embeddedness in the group seems to offer a weaker substitute for attachment to a specific person.

Amia: I have one story about attachment to a peer, to a friend, and it comes from a man who is in one of my therapy groups. Although I had very good interviews in my research, I don't think I got to this level in them. Toward the end of a year-long Gestalt group, one of the men said that he wanted to speak about fear of abandonment. He immediately started to cry, and when he managed to speak, after crying for a long time (and you know that men in Israel don't cry very often), he started to tell me that he is kibbutz-raised from a kibbutz with common sleeping arrangements.

When he was a tiny child, there used to be nights when the hyenas would come and howl, and the children would be in terrible panic that they were approaching. He got into the habit of sneaking into bed with one little boy. They would hug each other and sleep, and every morning they would be found in this bed together. This went on for years and years, and, he says, this was the only way that he could stand it, when his parents left him in the children's home at night, to know that this other boy would be sleeping with him.

The second stage of this story was when the two served in the military together during the Lebanon war, and suddenly he heard that his friend was wounded. He tried to go and find him and see how badly he was wounded and help him. But he had his own job in the military, in a different unit, and he was not allowed to go. He got into some sort of a quarrel with his commander and said "I must go! I must see my buddy, I must go and save him, I must go and see, maybe he needs blood, maybe he needs something!" He was not allowed to go. The other friend survived, but the main point is the shock that my group member got from realizing how intense this attachment was.

The third stage of the story is that now this man is a father. Every night, to make his little boy go to sleep, he crawls in bed with him and they go to sleep together. He says,

> Then my wife comes and wakes me up at 9 o'clock, half past nine. I take a nap and fall asleep with my little boy. I think he will never know how to fall asleep alone, because I tell him a story, I lie down with him, and we fall asleep together.

All this came up around the termination of the group, with the sense of being deserted or abandoned when we leave him. He attributed a lot of his need not to be abandoned to being raised in the common sleeping arrangement. He feels that every individual who went through the experience of being left alone for the night in the children's home must carry this feeling. But only he, because he's in psychoanalysis and group therapy and a clinical psychology student, can really go back and admit it and talk about it.

Ruthellen: That really does bring us to the summary. Different ways of looking at the attachment puzzle seem to come up with different facets of experience. If you look at it clinically, you certainly do find these imagined fears and this kind of tremendous terror about being deserted, and so on, but that's looking at it clinically. The question is: Do these people come for clinical help because they are carrying this difficulty? If we look at it intensively, as I have with people (and some of my participants have been in therapy), most of them don't talk about abandonment fears to any greater extent than those people who weren't communally raised. It's not that they don't mention them at all, but then people who weren't communally raised have abandonment depression and worries also. I don't hear a real difference in that.

I do hear more security in the holding dimension from people who were communally raised, in the sense of having people to fall back on. People raised in nuclear families often feel that all they have is their parents: If I don't have them, then what else is there? Their tremendous amount of anxiety about lapses in the relationship leads them to make many more demands on the relationship.

Ruth: Well, the opposite model, the model that I think nowadays is replacing the psychoanalytic one, says that the more secure you are with your parents, the more you can use the security of others as an extension. I think, then, if we go to attachment theory, supporters of this model would say that many subjects cannot talk about abandonment because they have healed this open wound by closing it.

Hadas: I think it also depends on what kind of message the parent gives the child. One girl whom I interviewed told me that because her mother was city raised, her mother was different from the other mothers. She was much more caring, she was much more attached. So it's also the whole message that goes with it.

Ruth: Yes, I agree.

Amia: But I agree with you, Ruthellen. If I would summarize these two sections, I would say that in terms of holding, there seem to be some advantages in the basic experience of kibbutz child-raising. However, in the attachment area, we have a lot more negative examples, problems in the creation of attachment.

Ruthellen: We still have a lot of confusion about what attachment really is, and I think this is, in part, because we don't yet know how to say what attachment is in adulthood or in adolescence.

Ruth: In terms of my background, I go back to the Harlows and their many studies, in which they essentially tried to see the corrective effect of being raised with peers when you are not raised with parents (see, e.g., Harlow & Harlow, 1966; Harlow, 1963). They had what they called the "security choo-choo train," in which little monkeys raised only with peers would cling to each other when they were frightened, and that was their form of security base. Thus, they exhibited attachment behavior, defined as clinging, in a situation of fright. The Harlows had conflicting findings. In some of their studies, they said, "Yes, peers can be a corrective experience for the parentless." However, in another article, they softened their conclusion and wrote that peers and parents have different functions, but functions that overlap.

6 PASSIONS

Amia: The funny part about this dimension is how the early kibbutz movement tried to abolish passion within the couple, and leaders really felt as if they could at least postpone it. They didn't know how to integrate the great emotional investment between two people with the total loyalty and total commitment to a group of people they demanded. This is where the Buber quotation seems to be especially relevant, where it seems as if there is a limited amount of loyalty or love or commitment within a person, and if you give it to the couple, you will immediately break the collective.

It also calls to my mind stories in the earlier kibbutzim diaries about the triangles that were formed. There were more men than women in the earlier groups because the commune was built on a lot of physical labor, and women were not easily attracted to or accepted by these early groups. Tzur (1988) has stories about the tremendous agony of jealousy one man felt being rejected by this woman who goes out with another, and men crying, and men breaking down, and suicides based on romantic issues in the very, very early kibbutzim. All kibbutzim have mysterious early suicides in their history, and many are based on passion and unreciprocal love relationships and so on.

So these are the myths of the kibbutz, and Ruth was right in asking if the kibbutz leaders ever claimed that the way to regulate sex life would be to open the society to some sort of completely free love. At least today (I mean the last 20 years, since I've been studying kibbutzim), they all say it never reached this point. When the solution seemed to be free love, they preferred to go back to the monogamous couple and allow for a family to form, with some reservations. For instance, kibbutzim didn't get into religious ceremonies of marriage, and they often didn't even let the couple live alone in a room but added on a third person. Leaders would see it as not normative for couples to walk together, to take trips together—they would always ask the couple to add others to the couple relationship. But sex was limited to the couple, and when a man and woman had a child, they were always recognized as the biological parents of the child.

So passion was accepted as something you should put boundaries on. In that, kibbutz leaders often quoted Freud, and they said that all the unfortunate results of "civilization and its discontents" come from the normal way that sex life goes on. That if you can really tailor it to a more advanced and more—

Ruth: Sublimate it?

Amia: They had a feeling of maybe having a lesson to learn from Freud about conducting sex life in a more enlightened, open-minded, modern way.

Ruth: I thought that this was the basis for having a more free attitude toward sex.

Amia: But this was never fully accepted. So the kibbutzim had to shape the couple relationship as less exclusive.

Ruthellen: Most utopian societies, I think, have come up with this idea, because the utopian society, by definition, is egalitarian: Everyone is the same, we all share. We don't have to deal with these painful differences that go on in validation, because if you allow each person to be seen uniquely, then some people are going to be better than other people, and some people are going to be liked better than other people, and then you have to deal with competition and envy and greed, and all of these other horrible human characteristics that come from the fact that we were born different.

How this is meaningful in passion is in what Amia called exclusivity—that if you allow strong couple bonds, then one person is going to choose another, and in choosing another, implicitly reject everybody else. And if you choose somebody else intensely, then you might want to possess the other person, you might want them all to yourself, and that also flies in the face of the utopian ideal, where everybody is supposed to be the same, and we're all supposed to be equal. There's no room, then, for certain people to be more special than other people, and that seems to be the painful rub here. Bettelheim said that what the kibbutz tried to do in order to decrease this process was, in effect, to make sex less exciting, less interesting, and the philosophy around raising boys and girls together was that they should get so used to each other that—

Amia: We'll talk about children in a moment. But one more comment about the grownups, the younger people who were the founders. When they formed relationships, there was very little consideration of their needs for privacy and for ongoing space and opportunity to develop their couplehood. There is the story of Na'ama, whose husband was very active in the Hagana, so for years and years he was absent; he was sent abroad to organize illegal immigration. It never occurred to the kibbutz leaders that the wife was perhaps longing for him and should go with him. Later, he was sought by the British police, so they put him in hiding in a different kibbutz, under a different name, and she was not allowed to join him. She could visit under very limited circumstances, once every 4 weeks. At the end, this woman really made a big scandal. She said "I want to live with him! We are married now for 4 years or so, and we never had a chance to live together!" The leaders allowed them both to join another kibbutz under different names, so they made the minimal understanding step toward this couple. Although not all of the stories were so extreme, there was no understanding of this attachment. People thought that the kibbutz and the group were kind of a replacement for this emotional tie.

Ruth: In the kibbutz, the personal takes second place to the communal. Take the relationship with babies, for example: *personal, self-interest*, or *selfish* were the labels put on such emotions. Another aspect, which I think is different for different generations, is the whole issue of sex within the peer group. Part of the late Joseph Shepher's (1971) research showed there were few marriages within the nuclear peer group and maybe not even sexual relationships.

Amia: How many weddings really took place among people who grew up in the same peer group? The answer is very, very few. Tiger and Shepher (1975) implied that the peer group, because of communal upbringing, creates a taboo on sexuality similar to the taboo on sexuality within the family.

Ruth: Marriage statistics are more readily available. However, some groups do experiment sexually. The stories are that as soon as it gets dark, children are active, and the absence of adult supervision enables various adolescent activities. So I think that this generation is different, or we are getting more open information.

Amia: But in my book, you still have quotations like this one:

> The class you grow up with develops unusually close relationships, very much like a family, like brothers and sisters. It is very difficult to explain to anyone who hasn't grown up on a kibbutz. These people have shared rooms and showers with me since we were babies. It's a very strong feeling. Therefore, I cannot consider having a sexual relationship or a love relationship with one of the people in my group.

So they keep saying it, and I know that I saw the statistics, which say that intimate relationships in the peer group are very rare. If they occur it is a secret, and they will not develop into a couple that is known publicly.

A love affair or a sexual relationship will rarely occur within the class. Perhaps a class is indeed more like a family. This girl herself feels that it's like incest. But it's true that lately people speak also much more about incest than they used to.

Ruth: Yes, that's an interesting comment. We don't know if it's flourishing now or if people are just talking about it, but we didn't hear about this much incest 10 years ago, and I think it's exactly parallel. The issue of sexuality, as well as abuse within the family, has been exposed in the last 15 years in the United States and the West, with the implication that it was there all along. Remember the recent claim that Freud both discovered and then covered the issue of sex within the family. He proposed that these were his patients' fantasies.

Ruthellen: I have one participant who tells a story about what happened when he was 10. He was from one of the kibbutzim where they lived with the other sex. One of the people who was very important to him was a girl who was 2 years older, whom he shared a room with. She was one of his first intimate friends; he could talk to her about his feelings, and she could talk to him about hers. They actually lived together for 4 years, and he was very close to her, and lots of times at night they would have these long discussions.

> We discussed a lot of things. It was flattering. She had the personality of someone you could talk with, without being afraid that she would hurt me with it, that she would talk about me behind my back. And she would also talk to me about her concerns.

They stayed close, even after they left the kibbutz, and he married, and she married. Just before he went out of the country for a job, just before he left, when they were 35, she told him that all those years she had loved him but was never able to say so. And her dream had been to live with him someday, but she was so afraid of telling him about her fantasies, she was afraid it would ruin the relationship. And he then told her that he had had similar fantasies, but that he thought that he was too young for her, because he was 2 years younger, and he didn't think that she would ever be interested in him as a boyfriend. So they ended up with this shared fantasy, that they might have had this wonderful love relationship, but that somehow the experience of having lived together for 4 years as children made it impossible for them to speak about it.

Hadas: I think there is even today concern about the distance between people, the space. First of all, in my sample, as well, it's not customary to go around the kibbutz grounds hugging your boyfriend or showing physical affection. Even in same-sex friendships, there were a few girls who said that you could never touch one of the girls in your group. One of them said that now that she has had interaction with city girls, when she sees them, she hugs them, she gives them a kiss. She said you would never do that with a girl from your group, even though you feel this tremendous closeness.

When I asked her about it, she said it's just a "city girl way of behaving," and you wouldn't want to behave like a city girl. But also it's as if it was going to be viewed as showing lesbian inclinations. It seems that something was very frightening for them about showing physical affection, both on the outside and also within their group of girls. Somehow it was threatening.

Amia: Yet sexual relationships are rather prevalent, but between classes. A teenager that I interviewed says,

> Sexual relationships between adolescents have become fairly common. This is an area which strict social norms didn't refer to, and people naturally did what they liked. It seems to me that we grew up with sex. It was always accepted and natural. There was nothing to hide, gossip about, or frown about. Girls were entitled to as much sexual freedom as boys. Although some people are still not at all open about it. A girl can ask for the pill at the clinic, or through her mother or the metapelet. They would all supply it on request without any questions. There is nothing to it, really.

Maybe it's superficial sex, I don't know. She's not speaking about love here, she's not speaking about any depth, but it sounds fairly easy and normal, except not within your peer group. It's usually with outside people, with people from the *ulpan* [Hebrew intensive course], for example. I'm speaking now about teenagers. They are very permissive.

Ruthellen: The environment is permissive, but it's not exciting. It doesn't seem very charged.

Amia: They really didn't tell me. I was not exploring that issue. I don't know, but maybe you're right.

Hadas: I was just thinking that it does seem that a lot of their needs are channeled to the passions, such as sexual relations with the opposite sex. I don't know if it's intimacy—

Amia: No, but here I think you're speaking about your sample of 25 to 30 individuals who were single. So for them the search for a partner, for formation of a couple, is really the major issue. I think that this is not representative of the kibbutz mentality at large. But in our joint study, we located people who were under great pressure to finally form a couple and have a child. I didn't ever feel that they were very highly charged in the sexual area.

Ruth: Throughout Western societies, I think that part of the main import of freeing women was that sex couldn't bind you in a relationship. It is as though a pendulum were swinging in the direction of having sex without the attachments, the investment, or the commitment, and I think that women needed that for a period of time to abolish the double standard. In an analogous way, the acceptance of free sexual behavior in the kibbutz may have served the function of diluting intimacy. Having sex does not express or create specific intimacy.

Amia: With all the areas in which women were *not* liberated in the kibbutz, you are saying they were liberated in the sexual area?

Ruth: I mean the larger society. It doesn't mean that individually, we don't see the same range that we saw before. But now people who are studying close relationships find that women are wondering if they didn't throw out the baby with the bathwater, wondering: Where is the connectedness? Do we really want this empty sex, which is free but not really meaningful? Maybe there are analogous processes going on in the kibbutz, in that there was the puritan period, followed by a free-sex period. Intimacy or commitment can still be missing as an aspect of sexual relations. I think that in history, there are always different opinions as to when it goes together.

Amia: It's funny to theorize that what happened on the kibbutz is part of what happened in the general attitude of women toward sex, because feminist ideology didn't catch up with the kibbutz women, or at least not very much. To say that this ideology was important in the sexual area, at least when the girls were teenagers, and they allowed themselves much more sexual freedom.... Maybe what this girl is saying is part of being rural: We grow up with sex, we see it in the animals, we see it as part of normal, natural life, and we are the same. I think this is more what she meant than some expression of feminist ideology.

Ruthellen: I don't see very much difference between my kibbutz sample and the nonkibbutz sample in terms of their sexual attitudes and passionate involvement. There are obviously passionate stories and nonpassionate stories in both. I do see that there is more permissiveness in the kibbutz, because the people seem to be free to bring someone of the opposite sex home to their room, whatever, for premarital sex, and extramarital sex also.

Ruth: I'm interested in the contradictory messages within the kibbutz society. Extramarital relations can be an equalizing and diffusing factor in close relationships. However, they may be a tremendous threat in a closed society. For extramarital sex, is there the same permissiveness in the kibbutz?

Ruthellen: Well, at least it's all known, you can't hide anything. People's extramarital affairs in the kibbutz all come to light, although they may have started out secret. Whereas there are secret extramarital affairs among those outside of the kibbutz. But how the kibbutz reacts to the affair gets very complicated. In some instances, the kibbutz simply learned to live with the affair—somebody just goes and spends nights with another person. But it is a source of gossip, and still something people get very interested in and talk about and deal with, and it makes everyone anxious, and so on. It's a matter of how you contain sexuality within an enclosed community, and it seems that the kibbutz even tried to deal with it by allowing whatever happened.

Ruth: The permissiveness is their way of containing it, as opposed to small communities, which would probably exorcise the offender.

Ruthellen: Because that would propel the people out of the community. Then, what would happen is that people who got passionately involved would have to leave, or they might blow the whole community apart, if you let people take sides. I think that some of what we're calling permissiveness comes from the fact that even those who are now raised in their parents' home still move out at age 16.

Amia: Maybe even 12. In different kibbutzim, there are different ages at which they move to the dormitories, living together. It depends.

Ruthellen: I don't know about those who moved out at 12, but the ones who grew up in kibbutzim with their parents still had a different experience from the city kids. In the city, the trend is for kids to stay at home much, much longer, because they can't afford to move out. Now they're staying well into their 20s, at least in the United States, where people are living at home until they can afford to get their own place. On the kibbutz, they have their own room, they can bring home boyfriends and girlfriends, and that seems to be all right.

Amia: But they share rooms, so it's a little more complicated. They have to make arrangements.

Hadas: I interviewed an adolescent couple who got a hut for themselves, and they lived there for 2 years, and no one minded.

Amia: Also, many of the Shomer HaTsair kibbutzim have a *mosad* (educational institute), which is a high school dormitory, and all the children from the different kibbutzim in the area come and live together, and they go home only for Shabbat. It's like a boarding school. They form new groups with people from new kibbutzim, and there is a lot of sexual activity going on, and the grownups know about it, and what they want is only to prevent pregnancies. As long as sex takes place with agreement, it's not a problem.

Hadas: Don't you think it's related also to the fact that there is less rebellion against parents, like the scenario of wanting to have sex when your parents don't want you to? That issue isn't as salient in the kibbutz.

Amia: They rebel against the ideology. They don't rebel through sex.

Ruthellen: By not getting upset about adolescent sexuality, what the parents are also doing is not pushing people together as a couple. This still prevents the exclusivity and possessiveness. By treating adolescent sexuality as something simple, it keeps people from taking these relationships too seriously, which is probably why I don't hear about them so much in the relationship space. They'll say, "you know, I had some girlfriends or boyfriends in there, but they were people who weren't terribly emotionally meaningful."

Perhaps one of the things that the parent generation is trying to do is to keep the kids from having relationships that are too emotionally charged and might not fit the larger context of the kibbutz. They want them to choose a permanent partner who will fit in to the kibbutz, rather than to become passionately involved with somebody who might carry them off. A number of people talk about falling in love with someone who came to the kibbutz and wasn't suitable or appropriate, and then being really stuck in a conflict with the kibbutz, not about the sexuality, but about the possibility they might leave.

Amia: Some of them are non-Jewish, coming on ulpan.

Ruth: Do you feel that the commitment aspect is embedded in these eight dimensions?

Ruthellen: I think it's in different places. I think that the focus on not being possessive or exclusive tends to militate against commitment on this dimension of passion, which is what we usually think of as being a critical dimension in modern day marriage outside the kibbutz. Not in all societies, but at least that's the current mythology: You fall in love with someone, and it's something about this special connection and the uniqueness of a loved person that keeps the couple together.

It seems to me in understanding the kibbutz marriages—I've talked to people, and in some cases, to both sides of a couple—that embeddedness is most important. The commitment is to the community, it's a joint commitment on the part of the couple to the community, and what holds them together is this commitment to their coupledom within this community, rather than to what's taking place between them. It's a role-related kind of commitment, but a role within the kibbutz ideology, within the embeddedness. Then the question becomes what happens when one or the other does have a more passionate experience with somebody else. That's where the extramarital issue comes in. I don't have an instance where a marriage broke up over that. It's always somehow contained within this community. People come to deal with it.

Ruth: I think that in the statistics quoted in an article by Kaffman, Shoham, Palgi, and Rosner (1986) about divorce in the kibbutz, I remember a figure relating to extramarital relations as one of the major factors in breaking relationships, which, again, just says that it exists.

Amia: I have an interview with people who were divorced, and I discussed divorce in the kibbutz with them. They said that because the kibbutz family is free from a lot of economic obligations to each other, problems of common property, alimony, or keeping your children economically secure, it makes divorce a much easier decision. I'll read it to you, it was a woman who was already 70 at the time I interviewed her, and she had been one of the first divorced women in the kibbutz. She never remarried, whereas her ex-husband married another woman, and they all live in the same kibbutz and are on quite friendly terms today. She says,

One difference between the family unit in the kibbutz and the conventional unit is that family relationships are not maintained for formal or technical reasons alone. Due to financial security within the kibbutz, families don't try to preserve their unity when the relationship has gone sour. There is no need to retain a framework which has become meaningless because of considerations of common property, livelihood, child care, and so on. It's quite easy to move out of your family room without otherwise disrupting your general lifestyle.

So the decision to be married or divorced becomes a highly personal decision. She's not speaking about love very directly, but I guess that what she says is that you don't keep on with a relationship when it's not justified by love. I don't know how popular this is.

Ruthellen: I have a number of couples in my sample which are definitely empty couples.

Amia: She says that false relationships are relatively rare in the kibbutz community. I don't know.

Hadas: Rabin and Beit-Hallahmi (1982) found less sentiment about marriage among the kibbutz couples compared to the moshav couples, as far as expression.

Ruthellen: There's less expectation about intimacy in some of these people. There are also intimate marriages—it's not all one or the other—but again, my sample isn't big enough to really make statistical comparisons. My sense is that it's not any different from the nonkibbutz world. There are empty marriages; there are committed and intimate marriages.

Ruth: I would just wonder about the role of social pressure, because I think that somehow the climate of our discussion was that divorce should be easier in the kibbutz. Without saying if it's more or less difficult—and I'm not sure, because I think that it has impact on your total life—a divorce in the kibbutz would still affect your workplace, your friends, where you sit in the dining room. It complicates your life. There are people who can work it out better than others. The individual differences are always going to be there, but I think that this part must be very hard.

Hadas: There was one girl among my interviewees, her parents divorced when she was 7, and it was very traumatic. She used to lie about it, and she had the sense of being ashamed, and then her mother even left Israel with this man. But maybe today there is more tolerance for it.

Ruth: Again, I think that divorce as a norm is not more acceptable than it used to be.

Ruthellen: But it gets complicated. Does one person then have to leave the kibbutz, or do both people stay on the kibbutz?

Ruth: There are different styles. Some people feel forced out of the community because they cannot bear either the real reflection or the imagined reflection, and some stay.

Ruthellen: One of my participants, in fact, had written a newspaper article about these complexities. This is a man who had an affair with his wife's best friend, who was also the teacher of his children in the high school.

Ruth: That summarizes the kibbutz situation: the social enmeshment. The lack of compartmentalization of aspects of life, workplace versus my parents versus my friends from college, and so on.

Ruthellen: Yes. At the same time, his wife was having an affair with a man who was a kind of kibbutz manager. It was known to some people and not other people, but it was extremely complicated. Everybody has multiple relationships with everybody else, and so if the passionate feelings aren't well-contained somehow by the social structure, things get out of hand.

Amia: Yes, there is a story here told from the point of view of the woman, and it was told also by others, and it is some scandal that has really shaken up the community very badly. The story is about a man and a woman, a couple. The man was very central, he was in charge of the cow shed, which was a big branch and a very important one, and his wife developed an affair with another man, and it became known, and they decided to separate. She was obviously going to live with this new lover of hers, to marry him or not, but the husband made a condition, that he will not stand it that she live with another man in this kibbutz, so if she wants to get an apartment together and make this relationship public, she has to leave the kibbutz, and if not, he will leave the kibbutz.

This was a much bigger threat for the kibbutz. He was a more prominent member, at least as his wife tells it, as part of a discrimination against women, because he was such an important member and had already been a secretary before, so they put pressure on her either to give up this love relationship or to leave with the man and live with him outside. From then on, her life became very messy, because she left, and she went to the Faculty of Agriculture to study, and she came back, and she left again, and she was really never able to live peacefully with her lover in the kibbutz. In fact, their relationship was interrupted by the community.

Ruthellen: Maybe one theme of all of this thinking is about the way ideology can influence relationships. It seems like there is a limit to that, at least to how much ideology can influence relationships when there is a special community embedded in a larger society. If this was an ideology of the whole society of a large country, we might see something quite different. But at least in the context of having a kibbutz within a larger society with somewhat different values, it seems that what the founders intended to do was really quite different from what turned out, and that at least in this dimension things look pretty much the same across the boundary between the kibbutz and the outside.

7 EYE-TO-EYE VALIDATION

Ruthellen: Let's talk about validation, eye-to-eye validation, with the negative pole being annihilation and rejection, and excess being transparency. I think that this is a very central dimension of what people talk about, maybe in all experience, but particularly in the kibbutz experience. Of all the dimensions, this is where kibbutz members seem to locate the most pain and the most frustration.

Amia: So maybe you want to talk about it, because in my experience, it is mutuality and embeddedness that they are more clear about. I didn't know exactly what eye-to-eye validation meant in the context of the kibbutz. Maybe I put it under a different heading. If you start, we will see.

Ruthellen: What is critical here, in terms of what people talked about, is that everybody needs to learn about who they uniquely and specifically are, and the only way to do that is by seeing one's self reflected to some extent in other people. Many of the people who grew up in the kibbutzim say they were so much a part of a group that it was very hard to learn about who they uniquely were. They were treated as a group so much of the time, and part of the group so much of the time, that although they may have felt both held and embedded because of the group, it was hard to discover their own specific qualities. This seemed to come out in a number of ways.

First of all, a number of people talk about difficulty just in learning about what their own feelings were. They felt they had been instructed in one way or another for such a long time about how they ought to feel—and how good kibbutz members feel—that they didn't have very much experience of being mirrored for their own unique feelings. This may be something, even more so than attachment, that is lacking when there is no ongoing and constant relationship with parents. The people I talked to seemed able to feel attached to their parents, but they didn't feel that their feelings were recognized.

Nor did they experience empathy, having another human being know how they were feeling in the moment, what their needs were, what their fantasies were, what their wishes were, whether their needs were met or not. Simply having that known, so they could identify a deeper or core self. I can describe a number of cases of people who in adolescence and in adulthood really had to struggle with trying to discover their own sense of self-experience. They had a feeling that they had been deprived of this all along, because they had been "good" kibbutz members, good children, good group members, good kids, good everything, and hadn't ever really had a chance to know themselves by their own name.

Ruth: I think that for me, we're talking about two things that are central to intimacy. One is to recognize emotions in yourself and accept them at some level, and the other is to be able, therefore, to reflect, to express toward others your feelings. In our studies, for example (Regev et al., 1980), we found that kibbutz children from the communal sleeping arrangement expressed less emotion toward their significant others, in comparison to children raised in the family sleeping arrangement and in the city.

In another study, by Arnon at Tel Aviv University (supervised by the late Sophie Kav Venaki and myself), we tried to assess the expression of a wide range of emotions. In both studies, we found communal kibbutz children more frequently avoided emotional expression. My thesis is that if you express your feelings freely, it's in contradiction to being so closely knit with others. The same closeness that you look for in other contexts by talking to people, I think in the kibbutz you have to guard yourself against.

Of course, there may be additional interpretations explaining the restricted expression of emotions, such as personality or situation or norms. In my first encounter with the kibbutz, when I was doing some kind of pretesting and interviewing kids, I came across the whole "gossip norm" in the kibbutz. I think this has to be a central consideration, and I think Amia talked about hearing from her subjects later that they felt exposed.

Ruthellen: Because you might get identified or you might get known—

Amia: Is expression of emotions under this heading?

Ruthellen: It's not just for the sake of expressing emotions. What Ruth is saying is that there are two pieces. In order to know yourself you have to know that you're being recognized in the sense of being validated. Early on, the baby who is joyful about finding some nice flowers may have a mother who will say, "Oh, aren't those pretty flowers," validating this child's awareness and enjoyment of the flowers. If nobody is there to do that, you don't really have the concrete sense that the feeling belongs to you, and that it can be known and recognized in the outside world. Instead, it becomes a kind of vague muddle, or it may feel like it's just part of a group enjoying the flowers. You don't really have the sense that it's a feeling that belongs to yourself.

That's what Kohut talks about as the sense of being mirrored and empathized with. There is a sense that what's inner has to be recognized by what's outer for it to be truly felt and integrated. One can express feelings that one knows about for the purpose of sharing them, and the joy of sharing them comes closer to mutuality. However, to be validated and to be known means that the other person simply hears you, recognizes who you are.

One of the ways that this fits very much with what Ruth was saying is that part of the fear of those people who do open up their feelings is that if they share them, this will be known by everybody, and they will get stuck with this label. It becomes public and usually misunderstood. The question is whether the communal situation allows for a real identification of one's sense of who one is, the feeling of being recognized and known.

The other level is what it means to live in a small community and to be so known, in the sense of potentially labeled by anything one does. This may hinder people's freedom of self-expression. Everything that they do is going to add to this label, including who their parents are, and this is one thing that links them to attachment, that this feeling of belonging to somebody leaks out on the validation dimension. So, for many people, their sense of who they are in the kibbutz derives from who their father is. The earliest sense of being known for these young people is "I am the son of my father" or "the daughter of my father" in this kibbutz setting.

That's more important than being who I am inside, because there isn't anybody who really wants to know who I am inside. Anything I do, which is part of who I am outside, is going to be known by everybody, and then there's going to be this image of me that's built. Once that is built over time, I'm going to be stuck with that, and no matter what I do, I'm not going to be able to get away from it. So when people then talk about their adolescent experience in the kibbutz, what they talk about is that wish to get away from this label, more than the people, or the kibbutz, or anything. They are suffocated by being identified in a certain way, through the experiences in the kibbutz, and that picture of them is etched in stone.

Amia: I have many quotations about this.

Ruthellen: I think we need to separate several things. One is just being known at all; second is being known in this labeling way; and the last way in which validation seems to become very important is the issue of being acceptable or not acceptable. People who feel acceptable in the kibbutz have very, very different experiences than people who feel unacceptable.

Ruth: Right. Bettelheim (1969) talks about the danger of having a false personality in the sense that people have to rely on your being a "good person," and an "adjusted" person. The luxury of either bursting out or acting out, or all the luxurious eruptions of emotions that you have in other contexts, including more chances to change or to be different things. Here you're really risking everything.

Ruthellen: There's a wonderful quotation from this one woman who struggled with this through her whole life, and what's interesting is how hard it is for her to get this into words. She says that when she was 10, there were some people she felt very close to, but she says,

> It was hard to feel really close to any specific person because we were so much of a group feeling, so you couldn't really be open and personal with people. It was just something, I don't know what it was, but there was something about expressing emotions that was stopped and blocked. I felt myself being closed up in a way, but we enjoyed being together. I always felt it was an ideal setting. I thought it was wonderful to be with friends doing interesting things together. When we were together, it would be a warm feeling of togetherness, but there wasn't the distinction of talking about personal things. I didn't feel that I could really know myself.

I think she's really trying to get into words that experience, that she felt the warmth, she felt the attachment, she felt the closeness, but what she couldn't get a hold of was a sense of distinction. Now she's in her late 20s, and in the past 8 years, she has been having relationships with people and experimenting with them to see how much she could share of herself. She's needed people simply to know her, not for anything else. Everybody is someone whom she either can talk to or can't talk to, and how much she can talk to them, and how much of herself she can bring forward, are important.

Amia: I have quotations regarding being somebody's child and not being a separate individual. The woman speaking is 29 years old. She says,

> I felt that in the kibbutz I would always remain "A and B's lovely daughter" and couldn't become a person in my own right. I know that had I stayed in the kibbutz long enough, I would probably eventually have received the chance to develop my own direction and personality, but I felt the need of an independent existence right away, and I sensed that this is much easier to achieve at a distance from my parents.

It is interesting that the same woman, when she talks about the common education, speaks about a mechanical way of treating the children.

She gives an example from the way children are given a shower at the children's home: "All the children passed through one after another like a factory. There is no personal attention, no warmth." Moving the children back home to sleep would certainly improve the situation.

So the idea is that you cannot define your uniqueness because you are either part of the common education peer group, constantly together, or because your parents—as founders, as important people in the community—kind of overshadow your separation as an individual. I think that with Hadas, 10 years later, we had many, many such quotations.

Hadas: Yes, it is the tension between the togetherness and the need to be distinct. There are four girls I interviewed who are from the same group, and I took each one's perspective about the group and about friendships. It's interesting that one of them said she didn't have "a girlfriend," and she used to switch whom she was most friendly with, and so forth, and then this other one says,

> I always had a close friend. I'm that kind of type who always needs someone by my side. If it was someone from my class, I like to have a deep relationship. Because I'm the youngest in my family and my parents are quite old, so I always felt that I needed someone to share with. It always bothered me that everything was so shallow. I also matured rather quickly and wasn't interested in all the petty things that I didn't like. We were 10 girls, so aside from the friendship, there were always wars and things that I didn't like, so I always chose a safe corner for myself, but on the other hand, I was active and sang, and so on.

They were 10 girls, and only three boys in the group, but, according to the girls, the boys were very weak. So this woman continues to say,

> I didn't always want to be part of the group, but to be me, individually, personally. We were very much a group together, but each of us as an individual on our own right was very different. Each of us is a different caliber, so it was good, because what really bothers me is that they always say that the kibbutzniks are all the same, and shallow, and in my opinion, it isn't true. Maybe it is true about some, but I didn't want it to be true of me.

So she said that each one picked a thing to stand out in, like each one played a different musical instrument. It reminds me of a big family.

Ruth: A family that stresses differentiation.

Hadas: She continues,

> Also, today we are very different, and each of us chose her own direction. There aren't even two girls who are going in the same direction, and because we were always looked upon as the group, and we were always together, maybe that's why each of us wanted to stand out and be unique in something. We were always this mass, these 10 girls. There were just three weak boys, and we controlled them, and we were witches to each other.

So I found here this real quest for uniqueness, even though on the kibbutz, their "groupness" was very much encouraged: That they are a good group, they're cohesive, that's a thing that the kibbutz appreciates. So this quest for uniqueness perhaps stemmed from the need to counteract the sense that for the kibbutz, they were an undifferentiated mass of "good girls." And then, as Amia said, we had a lot of examples of people talking about their image and so forth. It has to do with the total overlap of circles in kibbutz life. Many people say,

> You are born there. Everybody knows your parents, they know who you are, and you are this way because you belong to this family, and you are not another way because such and such, and there are your friends from your class, they have parents, and their parents are your parents' friends. So everybody knows everybody, and everybody knows everything about everybody.

Ruthellen: That's the transparency, that's getting to this excess of being known. Feeling invaded, feeling one doesn't have boundaries. Laing says that you can't become a person until you can keep a secret. That's the other side of validation.

Amia: They didn't even have a good way to know their gender. This quotation is from one of the first women born on the kibbutz. She says, "When we were growing up, boys and girls used to share rooms. We used to take showers together as long as we weren't ashamed, till we were about 10 or 11 years old." The idea was to stress the value of equality of all, including equality of the sexes. And then she tells about getting dressed in front of boys and how difficult it was.

> As one of my reactions I needed my privacy terribly. I used to retreat to the privacy of my mother's room. I didn't choose my roommates. I was always put with two messy boys so that the room might, thanks to me, retain some semblance of order. This was how the rooms were divided.

It sounds like not allowing space for any individual personality, neither feminine or masculine. And she says, "Personally I suffered from it. We lived in huts, boys and girls sharing rooms, and the togetherness was so intense, and I needed my own corner." I think that the corner is the idiom for "my own personality, my own space to develop as a different person."

Ruthellen: And to be recognized for that. For somebody to know who that person is in the corner, when it's coming from that person's own experience, rather than what's being put on them.

Amia: But some people enjoy this togetherness a lot. You also have people who say,

> I myself felt comfortable with this, with the noise and the constant social life. If you are an open person, and like your intense togetherness, then it's OK, but if you live on the margin of it all, you end up being rather miserable.

This young woman is from another generation, saying, "Living under each other's noses also means that we rarely have time to be alone. I personally don't mind, I'm glad to live closely with my friends, and I don't feel lonely." So they don't feel lonely, but they don't have a self, I think.

Ruth: That's Bettelheim's central theme.

Hadas: I found that, in terms of the capacity to be alone, which Winnicott (1958) writes about, after children raised on the kibbutz grow up and enter young adulthood away from the group, they really feel that they have to learn how to be alone because they haven't had a chance to do this while growing up. Away from the kibbutz, they are alone for the first time, and they enjoy it and want it. They feel that they have to master the ability to be alone in order to mature.

Ruth: The experience is one of having to work out the separation for the sake of your individuation.

Hadas: Here it's really primary. I feel that there are some people who were never, never alone.

Ruth: Perhaps they don't even know what the issue is. Is that what you're saying?

Hadas: But in a very extreme way. They've always been near people, and with people, never really faced being alone in the Winnicott sense.

Ruth: Yes. As a clinician, I would worry—and I would say that there are people who say, "I'm very social and positive," who haven't even met their unadjusted self or their angry self or whatever their private self is. Someone who assesses this by means of questionnaires and interviews would just find that the person says he liked the togetherness of the group and would like to continue to live with other people. So how do we reconcile the clinical and the social assessment?

Ruthellen: I guess it depends on whether it's working for them. One of the participants I interviewed is a young woman of 28. She was raised in a kibbutz, although she moved out of the children's house when she was just a year old. When she was 1 year old, they changed the arrangement, and so she lived with her parents. She's still living on the kibbutz, the same one, and when she talks about her adolescent experience, she talks about how she had a good place there. She was happy about how she was; she said she felt in the middle of everything:

> I didn't have to be worried about my place. I had friends, I was liked. When I think about that group, it meant having kids to play with, and not having to worry about being alone, or not being liked.

So she grew up with a sense of real continuity and closeness. Her life now is all about making a couple, and then making a family, all within the context of the kibbutz and the extended family. So she is very much the opposite of the first person I spoke about, who is very intent on finding a self and finding her uniqueness. This woman doesn't seem at all interested in that. One can ask if that's because she's denying it. . . .

Ruth: It sounds like she has a good life, as far as she feels.

Amia: I think that to be a unique individual was very difficult in the first stages of the kibbutz. Because the messages children received from both the family and the educational system were that you are all the same, there are no differences, you should do the same. So if your group is climbing the Gilboa mountain, but for you, it's terribly difficult, you should overcome it.

Ruth: Including sharing and rotating the use of clothing. Once your favorite shirt is here and once there. It's not the concrete aspect, but it's the metaphor, that you really weren't allowed to hold on, even to property that symbolically will connect you to something that is exclusively your own.

Hadas: And I guess a part of the context—or what you, Ruth, referred to as the ecology—is that even if the environment tried to foster uniqueness, still the other aspect, the sense of being stuck with an image, is almost inherent in the situation, the feeling that you're stuck with an image because you're staying in the same environment, where you grew up, where your parents are. There are a lot of people who say that only when they were outside of the kibbutz did they discover that they could be different, that they could choose who to be and how to be.

Ruth: It was a question that we raised before, but is this different, say, from an American small town, or from the experience of most kids who are in high school? You hear a lot of kids talking about having the same feeling in adolescence, that they were branded as something, that they weren't good at some kind of sport, and so they suffered terribly because other parts of them couldn't get recognized: They were only seen as lacking in some kind of ability. Then when they went out into a different environment and could get known again, they found that they could be seen by people in a different way and could then experience themselves very differently.

Amia: There was more flexibility almost everywhere than in the small kibbutzim of the 1950s and the earlier times, because there, you really were doomed to stay in the same group of people from the day you were born until you left for the army at 18. In every other community, you moved from junior high to high school, you had different schools, you could play with some neighbors who didn't go to your school. All this was missing in the kibbutz. They had these overlapping circles.

Hadas: It is more of a closed system; for example, in this quotation: "You feel closed from all directions. You know exactly what everyone thinks of you, so there is tension in the air, because in the kibbutz everyone knows everything about everyone. It's very stressful." That to me is more than just being a fat girl in high school that everyone perceives as "the fat girl."

Ruth: There was a study, a part of the Cornell–Tel Aviv project headed by the Bronfenbrenner-Shuval collaboration, in which I participated (Kav-Venaki, Levin, Esformes, & Karson, 1978). They asked kids who were in fifth, sixth, and seventh grade to describe their peers and themselves, using a long list of adjectives, positive and negative. They presented the same list to city and kibbutz children, a very large sample. Two of their findings are particularly interesting.

First, they found greater peer agreement (smaller standard deviations) in the descriptions of kibbutz children, compared to the descriptions of city children. Second, among the kibbutz children, the self-descriptions were more like the mean descriptions by peers. These findings may indicate that the kibbutz peer group knew each other much better than the city peers. However, it also indicates less freedom in perception both of self and others, and perhaps labeling as well, in the kibbutz. It is harder to escape one's image.

Ruthellen: People knew better, in other words.

Ruth: I chose to say that the descriptions fit better. As a youngster in fifth, sixth, or seventh grade, you don't always realize that you have a different perception of yourself. You really buy that label, you don't have the freedom to see yourself apart. So I think it was consensual but not necessarily indicating greater validity. This corroborates what Hadas was describing about the labels you receive, and in a self-fulfilling prophecy, you react in a way consistent with your label, so the whole picture becomes more static. Another aspect is that you feel like you are naked for a while. You have the feeling that people know you better.

Amia: We heard stories, I think in Hadas's material, about some parents who were for some reason outsiders in the kibbutz community—Holocaust survivors, I think, a woman that had a higher education. They were never integrated into the kibbutz society. Their son is telling us that his mother always encouraged him to be different, and she said to him, right away from early childhood, "you will not stay here. I'm staying here because of circumstances," and she did not encourage this conforming mode. The guy appreciates it, and he is really an individual, standing on his own two feet. He attributes this to his mother.

What she told him was not part of the common message. Usually parents said to children, "just conform," and they never had the security to go home and cry about wrongs done to them in the peer group or in school, because it was all one common front, the collective, and "I have to adjust." This was the only way.

Hadas: The feeling about "being known" in the kibbutz needs to be seen in the context of the fact that maybe you also feel less known by your parents, because they don't interact with you as much as parents and children do in the city. In other places, you can say to the teacher at school "you don't know my daughter, I know my daughter," but in the kibbutz, it may be different.

Ruth: Parents are part of the message—that's what Amia was saying also—they're not a different option. And maybe sometimes, they're just perceived this way. I'm not sure if it's true in reality that parents don't give different messages, but for the kids, it's like a unified front of adults, and you're really left on your own to deal with your peers. Using Vivian Seltzer's (1989) model of the healthy balance between relations with parents and peers, she would say that the parents' role is to provide the uniquely supportive aspect, which enables adolescents to carry on their struggle in what she calls the "peers arena."

Hadas: It's as if, in the case of the kibbutz, individuation develops later. What I found with the young people in their early 20s was that they sounded like maybe 14- or 15-year-olds, who are very concerned about how they're seen and, relatively speaking, they don't really know yet who they are uniquely. But it's not that it doesn't develop later, if they are in a situation that enables it.

Ruthellen: Some of it also has to do with the ideological commitment of the parents. In some instances, the parents were very much oriented to raising a good kibbutz member; this was the ideology. It's like the example you gave about the mother who stood outside and listened to her baby cry, telling herself that this was the way to raise a strong next generation. I had the sense, listening to some of these people talk about their parents that the parents were so focused on them being good kibbutzniks, they weren't so interested in them being good human beings, or being who they were.

I have one participant here who had an illness when he was young that was later diagnosed as polio, but it took them a long time to figure that out, so he was paralyzed for a while as a child, unable to walk. He was picked on by his group, people made fun of him, he never felt part of things. But, on the other hand, he was very bright and he did well in class. This was his strength. From an early time, because he felt so different from the kids in the kibbutz, he wanted to do something else, and his great act of rebellion against his parents was to want to go to college, to take the matriculation exams. They almost never forgave him for doing that.

This shows how hard it was to be unique on a positive side. In fact, he was only able to go to college because he was supported by a grandfather, who said to him, "Oh, do what you want to do, don't worry about these parents, don't worry about the group. You want to go to college, so go to college." So he was able to get that support from another generation. But his feeling was very much that he didn't fit, that he was different, and that what he was wasn't going to be recognized except for his difference, not for its strength or what it might be.

Ruth: I think it breaks down to two different aspects in my mind. One is a study by Miri Edelist (1980), supervised by Baruch Nevo, about creativity in the kibbutz. Kibbutzniks were found to be less creative on some standard creativity test. The other puzzle that I have is that part of the kibbutz education was very much to develop personal projects, and to use them as a basis for meaningful learning, some kind of open classroom teaching, which seems to go against what we are talking about, at least in terms of educational ideology: "Don't invest in grades, really pursue your own interests, do projects, and through the projects you will learn." I really wonder where all these messages have gone, what happened to them.

Amia: I think that people hesitate to admit that a school which is not competitive is very difficult to maintain in the long run. Kibbutz schools had a lot of dropouts, and they had very mediocre achievements. Once the members started to think about higher education and matriculation examinations, people started to work.

Hadas: In the student sample, I was impressed by their creativity, by their commitment to their studies.

Ruth: You were?

Hadas: Yes, because first of all, they have to do much more to get into university, and do the matriculation exams on their own after the army. Some people were very motivated. They would work a full day in the kibbutz, and then they would go to their room and study for their math exam.

Amia: We don't know what proportion of the kibbutz members this is, whether this is representative.

Ruth: Well, the question is, if we're interested in the average, or in consequences all along the scale. We see that there are some people who find their way to perform above and beyond the norm. I don't believe that you can stifle creativity. I think it's really like a current: The more stones that you put in the way, it just finds a different avenue.

Hadas: Yes, because it's interesting when you look at a certain group, such as the group of 10 girls I mentioned. There is one girl who says that, from a very young age, she wasn't interested in sitting out in front of the children's house and talking, and she always sat in her room and read books. She thought it was a waste of time to sit with the others. So you always wonder about the ones who somehow find their way to be different.

Ruth: Yes, I think some of the people who find their way to be different experience it as some agony. It's only in retrospect that they can appreciate their striving, not knowing why they were in that spot. I think if you're a kid, everyone wants to be like the others, popular, loved, and liked. While this is part of human nature, the kibbutz did encourage leveling. Students report efforts not to stand out in their group.

Amia: Being different is painful for children.

Hadas: Maybe in the kibbutz, the, so to speak, standard deviation that is allowed is so small that you have to do very little to be labeled deviant. In the sense that there are strict rules. I remember this one guy said, "If I feel like walking into the dining room with a tie, I can't do it, because it would be looked upon as crazy, whereas in the city, if I feel like putting on a tie, I'd put on a tie."

Ruthellen: I wonder sometimes if holding and validation aren't somehow opposed in some way. In the city, people are held less tightly, but they also have more of the freedom to be who they are. The other side of it is that they can also get lost more easily, that they may not be noticed at all by anyone. In the kibbutz, it doesn't sound like anybody gets completely lost because everybody at least has a label. Nobody can disappear in the kibbutz, as people can in the city.

I don't think I have had access to people who have disappeared, because people who aren't getting recognized at all are so much on the margins, so much on the fringe, that they only turn up later as deviants. People who become schizoid and completely isolated, people who fade so much from anybody's notice—this can happen in the city. In the kibbutz, that's not possible. Everyone has to be accounted for there somehow.

Amia: But it also has to do with embeddedness. Should we move to another dimension?

Ruthellen: It sounds like on validation, there's more agreement. All the different research points of view—from the clinical, the developmental, the social, and so on—seem to come closer to a notion that this is something that is very difficult for people to get on the kibbutz. It sounds like nobody brings up any counterevidence here. It seems that people universally report liking the kibbutz very much if they like the way that they are seen, or, what's even more common, people feel intensely uncomfortable about how they are viewed by others and then have to struggle with what to do about it, either to give up their difference and try to become the same, or to try to insist on the difference and see what happens.

8 IDEALIZATION AND IDENTIFICATION

Ruthellen: Next, we'll talk about idealization and identification, which is about people who represent ideals, values, or ways of being. Our question here would be, in what way are idealizations or processes of identification different in the kibbutz, and how is it that people come to connect to other people who represent or embody certain kinds of ideals that a person chooses to pattern their life on?

Amia: Well, since a kibbutz is built around certain ideas, it is different from almost any other type of settlement or town or neighborhood or whatever. The kibbutz is built around the ideology of equality, cooperative living, and reciprocal responsibility, and all these are not just phrases; all the kibbutz institutions are built around these concepts. So, the whole concept of ideology is extremely important in the awareness of relationships among people.

Also, the shift of the kibbutz between the different generations, I think, is most prominent on this dimension. I find it extremely meaningful. Every single story in my book makes some reference to this dimension. I can pick some of the most important ones. First of all, for the founders' generation, the needs of individual people and the relationships among them were secondary to the actualization of the ideas.

In fact, the term *actualization*, which psychologists use so much for a person's own needs and potentials, the founders used for creating a reality that follows their values, the kibbutz dream. Being so strongly identified with a certain set of values created a lot of conflicts as well. So in the first generation, you have two types of people. You have people who are terribly, terribly proud of themselves today, and say,

> We had the dream, but the reality is even better than the dream. We were walking in the early 1920s in the street of a little town in Holland, and we saw the nice little homes and the flowers on the windows, and we said "we will create a better universe," and indeed we did.

We can sense the self-esteem that comes from such feelings. The others are people who couldn't make it. They joined this community based on ideas, and then they found that it did not fit their personal makeup, or they could not cope with the physical labor, or they couldn't be successful members of this community in some other way. They were in a terrible impasse personally.

This is the background for the suicide stories. Many of the early suicides had to do with problems of values. For instance, there is a story here: "Some people couldn't take this kind of life. We had many suicides in the beginning. They started very early, approximately nine suicides in 9 years. Two or three of them nearly destroyed the community." I ask the speaker the reason for the suicides, and he says,

> It's difficult to understand the reasons for that kind of desperation, but in a very young society, the majority of the people were 18- or 19-year-olds, all of us had drastically changed our lifestyles, from the middle-class intellectuals to the homeless day laborers, often hungry and sick with fever. In the background was awareness that we needed to change our lives, and to change our type of careers and values; it was a profound inner struggle. Work was the highest value in life, yet work was terribly difficult physically, especially in that heat. In the kibbutz, a person was judged by his working ability, and some of the people who were used to being very popular before, and respected, suddenly were despised and scorned here, since they couldn't stand the difficult work, and this was one reason for the suicide, for example.

Idealization and Identification

So we see how values really not only surpassed people's relationships, but even their sheer existence. When this passes to the second generation and the third generation (and it's interesting to see how the children look at their parents), we deal with the question of identification. One of the daughters says,

> Frequently I envision my parents' generation as giants who will soon be gone, while we are dwarfs by comparison. All the things that they underwent and accomplished, I couldn't even cope with. They had fantastic will power, which I admire in them, and to this very day they haven't slowed down. My father, for example, still carries a tremendous load, although he's almost 70. He alone contributed to so many fields.

This goes on and on, a lot of admiration toward the parents' generation. Remember that this goes together with all the criticism on the personal level, but on the general level, it is a sort of idealization that I haven't seen in other places. Several of the people I interviewed speak about their parents as you speak about gods. There is somebody here— I can read a few sentences from her:

> When I think about my parents, and their generation, even realizing that they were partly the products of their era, I still admire them for their great ability to withstand physical and spiritual hardship. They were very strong and resilient people. On the other hand, take me for example, I really am so weak, I reacted so badly to the Yom Kippur War, it's a trauma that I'm still suffering from.

But again, talking about her parents, she says,

> These people have such fortitude in crises that are difficult to cope with. I regret not having their faith. It is good to live with such deep faith. I don't seem to be able to find any articles of belief in my generation, and they clearly had it. I have nothing to delineate a certain way of life.

So she compares the materialism of her age group with the attitudes of her parents, who seem to be above and beyond all this. I think that this is the major theme of life in the kibbutz, the way that you relate to values and the way you divide people into those who realized the values and those who betrayed them. And the young ones betrayed them, in a way.

Ruth: I think that is the main difference for me between people who joined the kibbutz and those who were born there, and I feel that those who joined effected their separation and individuation process by making a choice, by working for it, even by leaving their homes, in a sense. I think the paradox is that, in some respects, they're expecting the children to continue, not realizing that psychologically, as a model, they have been a model of people who broke away, who built a new thing, who individualized separately, to use your expression. They expect the children to continue whatever they have given them, and they don't see that, as Jane Loevinger (1959) said once, children do not only what you tell them, but also what you have *been* for them. As models, they are not models of continuous investment.

Amia: Of conformity?

Ruth: I don't want to say conformity, but even just to stay and continue the tradition. Maybe this can be invented by the children, that there is a tradition to be continued, maybe they can own it as their own, but I don't think that many of them are doing it. Members of the young generation, I think, have to make a choice of their own, and the kibbutz is one of the options. Luckily, I feel, it is no longer such a betrayal to at least explore other options outside of the kibbutz.

Amia: This is the third generation. I think that we have schematically three generations. The first generation was very committed to the ideology and really sacrificed a lot on the personal level, but when they look back on their lives, they are mostly quite content with what they did. This is the first generation very stereotypically—of course, there are differences.

The second generation was brought up under very austere, very difficult conditions, and its members grew up to become very good kibbutzniks and to perform all the duties and to be conforming, but they didn't incorporate the great belief, the great faith. If they left, they felt that they were betraying, and if they stayed, they stayed out of inertia. They didn't have this giant spiritual investment that their parents had, as Ruth says, justly so, because the parents created their own dream, their community.

Idealization and Identification

The third generation is more "normal." Its members don't follow up automatically: They are willing to express rejection of some things, they are willing to integrate other ideas, they are willing to test other lifestyles. Members of the second generation were under the shadow of their parents in such a tremendous way that they were paralyzed in many ways. But they were very successful economically. This was the avenue open to them, to be outstanding economically, but not in other ways.

Ruthellen: What I see in the third generation, those whom I've interviewed, is not a commitment to the content of either the parental or the grandparental ideals, but a real quest for something ideological. Ideology, in general, is very important to these people. They have to believe in something, and they seem to want to try to believe in something through finding someone who embodies what they want to believe in.

So there is a quest for people to look up to, and this is especially true among the men. It's also there in the women, but it's mainly true among the men. They'll talk about people being important to them because of the ideas that they represented. This seems to be true retrospectively, even from a very early age. That is, many people will represent someone on their diagram, even as early as 5, as someone whom they really looked up to or admired, the hero, the pilot. Many of the kibbutzim, for example, had a war hero of one sort or another who was very much admired and idolized within the kibbutz. Then at age 10 it would be someone, maybe a youth group leader, or an older person, who seemed to represent some kind of belief system that was very important.

I have one young man who ended up with a relational space at age 20 that seemed to just have people who represented different ideas. There was a cousin who was very important to him because the cousin was very religious; and then there was an older brother who was very important to him because he was very artistic; and then there was a cousin who was very important to him because she had joined the anthroposophic movement, which also had its own brand of ideals; and also there was his father, who represented the kibbutz ideology. And he experienced himself at age 20 as almost sitting back and watching these people struggle over the different ideals, so that he could know who was right, and what he could believe in. But he couldn't ever get to where it would be resolved. Each person representing a different ideal was pulling him in a different direction.

Then he went to university, and he was studying philosophy, when he met a professor who told him that values and ideals were on different levels, and he began reading a philosopher who said that you could never resolve the question of which ideal was best. Once he had that, he felt freed to believe in what he wanted to believe in, and then the importance of these other people as idealized figures began to fade. For the first time, he began to make other kinds of relationships with them, which he hadn't really done up to that point, because he had experienced them just as human incarnations of ideas. That's really all I could hear from him, or that's all he would talk about. He talked about the importance of people from his adolescence into his early adulthood as figures who represented ideals.

He was somewhat more extreme than other participants, but there were many—always male, kibbutz-raised people—who put on their diagrams authors, for example, or philosophers, or people whom they had an intense relationship with through their ideas, and in some instances, these people would be as important to them as family members. This is what raised the question that you mentioned before, Hadas, about the relationship between ideology and interpersonal life, because for some of these people, it was clear that ideology was a form of interpersonal relating. I don't so much see it as compensatory. They simply felt an intense connection with people around ideas. I think there is a gender difference here, because one piece of it that does connect to the nonkibbutz-raised sample is that men, in general, are more prone to talk about people as being important to them because of discussion or representation of ideas. It's very rare for women to say, "this person was important because we talked about this idea and we had an intellectual connection."

Hadas: They would say, "We talked about relationships."

Ruthellen: Well, "We talked about our feelings, we talked about our thoughts, we shared our beings." Ideas may have been a part of that, but to specify it as an intellectual relationship is extremely rare among women. I think that the ideological aspect is much stronger, as you say, with people raised in the kibbutz, whether it's following in the grandfather's footsteps, or in the father's footsteps.

Amia: Putting yourself vis-à-vis this is part of your identity. You must make a decision, or you must know you're in conflict, but the ideology is a very live part of one's personality.

Idealization and Identification

Ruthellen: Also, because in many instances, fathers are not as available or physically present, they're terribly important as carriers of an ideology. They're hard workers in the kibbutz, and people in the kibbutz seem much more sensitized to what fathers represent ideologically than people outside the kibbutz. When I asked people to tell me about their fathers, I was much more likely, in the kibbutz, to hear about the important work that the father had done, or the ideas that he carried, than outside of the kibbutz, where people would be more likely to say things like, "He was working very hard and he wasn't around very much," but not to talk about the importance of his work or the father as an idealized figure. In some instances, I do have a couple of women (these were all women who stayed very attached to the kibbutz, whether they live on it or not) who had fathers who were very important in the kibbutz, and therefore had a very strong tie to the ideology of the kibbutz, as a way of identifying with their father.

Another thing I heard from the kibbutz-raised sample that I didn't hear from the nonkibbutz-raised sample is the importance of older kids to represent the next step. This is another piece of the communal raising in the peer group. It's not only the peers that one is raised with, but a lot of people put the next level group on their relational maps as a sense of "that's where we're going." It's really a feeling that the path is somehow laid out for them, and they can look up a stage and see "that's where I'll be."

This was much more pronounced than in the nonkibbutz sample. The feeling that you could see in other people where you were going. The younger kids would look back and talk about how older kids were important. The sense was that they were models for them, and also that they often had older kids doing activities with the younger kids, and there were then a lot of possibilities for relationships of identification.

Ruth: I haven't really thought about this before. This seems to be a major channel for feeling the influence in the community, or representing the influence of the community. I think that in the city, you usually don't have such an entity to refer to. I was wondering what their thoughts were on the religious option. Were any people among the secular kibbutzim exploring religion?

Amia: Yes, they do. You know that among the cults, the percentage of kibbutzniks is much higher than you would expect from their proportion in the population.

Ruth: Then I think it really strengthens what I had in mind, that this represents in some way some of the belonging to the community, an identity of the community, some kind of an abstract value system, which really has implications for the way that you are going to live. It's not just ideology in some empty way, but it does dictate certain decisions. So I think that searching for religious or cult experiences is really keeping the structure of having something central influencing your life, looking up to it, or rebelling against it, but something very compelling. If it's not Lenin, than let it be the Guru. It goes back to previous discussions that there is an internalization of "the kibbutz" as a total community, and something greater than the individual claiming your total being.

Amia: Yes, that you should have this part of your relating, a very clear system of values.

Hadas: And if you throw out the old values, you have to find new ones. It's interesting, because there was this one kibbutz where they were discussing whether the kibbutz should fund a member's participation in the *Emin* [a cult based on a spiritual thesis and a way of life] as equivalent to university studies, which the kibbutz pays for. Of the young adults on this kibbutz that I interviewed, all of them mentioned the Emin issue.

How the old people were against it, and the young ones said, "No, you're not going to decide for us, and if I want to go to the Emin, I should be able to go to the Emin." So it looks like, as you're saying, for the younger generation, it can become an alternative channel for ideology.

Amia: This is a three-generation story. The grandmother is a woman who had really given up her love relationship because she was committed to an ideology. Her husband was going abroad all the time, doing things for the government, and she says, "We sacrificed a lot, but we were happy because we knew that we were doing something important." This is the first generation. Her daughter is the one I read to you from, who idolizes the parents so much, saying, "We are the midgets and they are the giants, I wish I had the faith to go by, I wish I had some way of life, and so on, I regret it."

And her granddaughter (from the third generation) left the kibbutz and went to live with an Emin community. Now the girl's mother, when she tells me about this, she says, "But she's happy, because she has again the frame of values that people need. I don't see how you can live without a system of beliefs which will tell you what's right and what's wrong."

Ruth: Remember that the first generation left nice Jewish homes in the small *shtetl* in eastern Europe, in which you knew where you went on Fridays and Saturdays and what you did on Passover.

Amia: But they created another one instead, a modern one.

Hadas: Another example of how much ideology is relational is when we interviewed people about loneliness, and they referred to loneliness in the context of ideological crisis. They said something like this, and it's not something I asked about, it came up spontaneously:

> There's loneliness in the very expectation that the community will achieve 100% of the Utopian ideals, and if it achieves only 20% (although these may be the 20% which really count), what ends up is a recognition that the perfect happiness, in which everyone is happy, isn't reached. It is so frustrating for the idealistic people, or those who try to accomplish this ideal, that it all actually looks worse than it really is.

This was said by a male, a kibbutz leaver. Then a kibbutznik who is on the kibbutz, also male, said,

> There is a different kind of loneliness, it is my father's generation of the 50-year-olds. It is more the loneliness of having done something all your life, fought for something and worked toward it, and suddenly there is a sort of feeling of loss. That with all this life of work and craziness of building something, and trying to maintain it, and there are many more problems on the kibbutz that were not anticipated, so they feel suddenly this loneliness. If you feel tied up and you want to do something to change it, but you know you can't, so you feel alone in the battlefield.

Ruthellen: I think that they are saying that ideas feel like company, something that you are attached to, like a person.

Amia: Yes, she says, "I feel a sense of loss and emptiness in our way of life." So without values, you are empty.

Ruthellen: But there is this personification of ideas, somehow turning a person into an idea. There's this easy transfer between what's personalized and what is ideologized. One of my interviewees is a woman whose father had built this kibbutz, and she idealized him and devoted her entire life to continuing his work, to carrying on the kibbutz and sacrificing everything to that, and she married and raised her children along the same lines, and it was very important. Then in her 50s, she had a crisis of tremendous disillusionment with the kibbutz movement, feeling that people weren't working as hard, people were thinking only about themselves, not thinking about other people. She had a personal crisis with the kibbutz in wanting another kind of apartment, which they had promised her and then didn't give to her, and she felt that her work had not been appreciated and that she wasn't being adequately acknowledged for what she had contributed.

Her sense was that the whole thing had gone sour, and it is for her, I think, this feeling of having, in some ultimate way, lost the important part of her father. What he stood for, what he carried for her, was not love, affection, validation, all these other kinds of things that we were talking about, but he carried an ideal, and the relationship was based on this joint commitment to the ideal. She was close to him and participated with him in carrying out these ideals. So when the ideals were crushed, she lost her father, too. She lost what she had of him—that's what the relationship really was about.

I think that I hear this also with many of the other people in the kibbutz who have connected strongly through an ideological basis, and I think that this is a more prominent dimension in those who are kibbutz-raised than those who are not.

Amia: Also, in making the decision to form a couple relationship, it is a thing that comes in. If I'm a kibbutz member, and I meet another person, will this person come with me to the kibbutz, or will we leave? So the decision to create a relationship is also confused, often, with the issue of where to go and which lifestyle to select. I think it is a much more prominent concern than among city people who form a relationship. When Hadas asked, what do you think about your future, will you go back to the kibbutz, many people said, "It depends on whether I find someone who is interested in living in the kibbutz."

Ruth: So the personal is taking the front seat in the present generation.

Idealization and Identification

Amia: Yes, it is a consideration when making choices.

Hadas: Also your career choices, your educational choices, every decision that you make has relevance to the decision whether or not you live in the kibbutz.

Amia: Whether it is for the kibbutz, or against the kibbutz.

Ruthellen: Well, that's what this person said, that she's raising her children to continue "our life in the kibbutz." She said,

> I said good and bad things about the kibbutz, but if you want them to continue the idealistic ways that your parents built for you, you have to show them the way, want them to stay in Israel, and to stay religious and to stay on the kibbutz, that's what's really important.

She lives on a religious kibbutz.

9 MUTUALITY AND RESONANCE

Amia: The kibbutz is very particular here, as well, in the sense that it develops a very externally oriented group life, with a lot of togetherness, but a life that is very shallow, artificial, that actually fights against intimacy, fights against the formation of deep friendships. It's like the passion dimension, but here regarding same-sex, or nonsexual relationships. The kibbutz norms fight against deep mutuality and maintain camaraderie and relationships and companionship on the superficial level. We have many quotations about it, and usually in the perspective of my interviews, they are phrased in the negative.

The negative attitudes are of two types: one is that people say they really longed for more intimate and deep relationships, and they didn't have the opportunity to develop them in the kibbutz, and the other negative concept is that group life was too crowded, too much invading one's privacy, that there was too much togetherness, so that I didn't have my own place to develop. I'll select some quotations:

> From the seventh grade on, which is when one joins the "children's society," children study, work, and must also be very active socially. Children work seriously here, doing a great part of the mass seasonal agriculture work. They also work hard preparing

101

cultural events. Every season has its holiday and the children's society must prepare for it. In the summer, it is summer camps, in the spring, it is field trips—it's an endless chain of social events, each one prepared to perfection, and in each one, you have to participate with the whole group.

You can never relax and be on your own. Of course there is homework and visits with your family, but you never have a moment for yourself. When you're finally in your room, it is shared with two other kids, and it's never quiet, it is very crowded in the children's dorm. That's why every kibbutz child dreams of the private room he or she will get upon returning from the army.

So this is a description that sounds judgmental, as I said, from the point of view of a 22-year-old girl raised in the kibbutz. Here's another, from a longer perspective, a 40-year-old woman looking back on the children's life in the commune:

For me the children's society was like a closed institution. I could never express what I felt, and I had only to be with them all the time. The same pressure works on adult members, the system wears people out, it makes them lifeless and mediocre.

The point is that you always have to be together, there is social pressure to be together and to conform to the norm. It looks like there is a lot of togetherness, but it's not a good togetherness.

Ruthellen: It's a kind of good togetherness. I think we have to discriminate the different levels here. Once they move on to discover another level, they're sort of talking about what they felt they missed earlier.

Amia: But it is pretty common in these records—I don't know, maybe I selected them this way—for them to say that there was a lot of togetherness, and that it was good at a very superficial level, but that there was a lot missing. And I think that the one who gave the best perspective is somebody who joined from the outside, an American woman, who made *Aliya* to the kibbutz as a grownup and married a kibbutz member. She's an English teacher in the kibbutz and now also a parent. Her husband is kibbutz born, she has students, she knows the other teachers, but still she maintains some sort of an outsider perspective. She says,

You must know, first of all, that I enjoy life here. Although I am critical, I like it. The only thing I really miss of the life I might have had in the States is friendship. It is a weird thing about the kibbutz, something that I've only discovered gradually, that kibbutz members don't develop intimate relationships among themselves.

In the States, I had very close women friends. We could talk about anything, and our relationships meant a great deal to us. Here I don't find this at all. One is close to one's family, but other relationships are very superficial. I myself am suited for that kind of relationship, and I have found a friend here, but significantly, she is also a new immigrant, a Swedish woman. My friendship with her is so important that it has changed my whole perspective on my life in the kibbutz, and I know that it has the same effect on her. I feel, however, that the kibbutz is somehow working against such a relationship. Real friendship is uncommon.

Unintentionally, the kibbutz stands in our way, although it is difficult to pinpoint how. The kibbutz is a network, in which everybody comes under scrutiny, while to develop closeness, one needs a bit of privacy, of secrecy, an atmosphere of romance. It is the same with love affairs. I don't want to sit in the dining hall and hear gossip about my closest friend. I want to have my own private image of her. This is a situation which is quite difficult to maintain.

This is a thing that she observes in her students, and she says,

My adolescent students don't form intimate friendships either. I believe it is a result of the tendency of kibbutz children to conform, not to deviate from the group in any way, not to enter into confrontation with anyone. When a friendship is formed, one must partially reject others, and this is a highly unpopular thing to do.

This has become a common observation in the literature about the kibbutz. But here the nonpsychologists, people who speak from their experience, express what I said generally before.

Ruth: I think that the whole issue of intimacy is now well-known, that it is more difficult and it's harder to find in the kibbutz. In one study with Asa Arnon (1978), we compared communal versus family settings: You find intimacy a little more in the family setting, which means that the separation in terms of where you sleep and the option of being with your parents does allow for certain aspects of friendship or intimacy to be there.

I think for me, the part that keeps haunting me, is the questionnaire I called *comradeships*. After I didn't find the same degree of intimacy with a single best friend, I was really hoping that I missed it, and I would find some kind of a general peer-group intimacy on dimensions like identifying with the group, or how important the group is. City children who described the kids they hang around with felt more positively about their group than kibbutz children felt about their primary group. The only aspect of comradeship that was more central for kibbutz children was the sanctions. This means that they felt more threatened, or more vulnerable, or that the peers were harsher. This finding supports a previous report in which kibbutz children experienced their peers in more negative ways than their city counterparts (Devereux et al., 1974).

I think that what you read to us right now is a very nice summary of how it is, and it's nice to see it from the perspective of someone who has been in both settings and knows what she's looking for, and she doesn't find that intimacy she's known. The other question is, is there any other form of intimacy, which for us nonkibbutzniks is less meaningful, and therefore we don't identify it, but it has a different name.

Amia: The holding that we discussed earlier.

Ruth: The holding is a replacement?

Ruthellen: I think it's a different kind of mutuality, I think that what you described is the sense that there are people there, that they always have companionship. There is always someone to be with, to go with, to do with, to live with. For city-raised children, or children raised in a nuclear family, the remarkable time is when they are with a friend, so they may go home and think, "OK, I spent the afternoon with a friend" or "I had dinner with a friend." For kibbutz children, on the other hand, I think the remarkable thing is any time when they are alone, or with parents. But when people spend all of their time in company, there may be some aspects that are just taken for granted. Having people around is like breathing air.

Mutuality and Resonance 105

Amia: It's like a marriage. I just heard a joke the other day that made it so clear. The customs officer is catching somebody, and one customs official asks the other, "How did you know they were smuggling things in?" And he says, "Look at this couple. They are probably married for 30 years, so what are they talking to each other so much about? So I was sure they were hiding something." People who are married to each other for 30 years don't need to talk. Perhaps on the kibbutz, too, there is this kind of feeling that there are people around, but nothing deeper than being together.

Hadas: I have a very good example of that. Mutuality is sharing, so there are two aspects. One is like Amia's joke about a couple married for a long time, and "Why are they talking?" Living together may make talking less important.

> When you're on the kibbutz, it's like you don't actually have anything to tell your friends. It's not like when you come back from the army on weekends. When we were in the army, we used to come back to the group, and there was a whole week that you didn't meet your friends, and you have a lot to tell, so many things happened to you, and you are always meeting new people. Here we're all in the same place, and actually the same things happen to all of us. So she works with the 1-year-olds, and I work with the 3-year-olds, so this one peed, and that one peed, what are we going to talk about? And then there are occasions when someone dies in the kibbutz, or we all see the same movie or show on Saturday night, and we speak to the same people and the events that life revolves around are the same.

The second aspect of not needing to talk is that you can't be mutual unless there are boundaries, also.

> In the kibbutz, you can't share with people, because in a kibbutz, loneliness is really total loneliness, precisely because of the tremendous physical contact. In the kibbutz, if a person runs into a problem, he can't talk about it with other people in the kibbutz. It immediately passes with the gossip from mouth to ear, and it develops. In the kibbutz, you cannot break through the image that there is of you, you can't escape it, so if you're lonely, it's total

loneliness. In the time of difficulty, you don't have [anyone] to whom to turn, except for your close family, but not other people, because you're afraid that somehow, somewhere it will return to you. This is something that is communicated to you so strongly, indirectly.

But there are other participants who say that there is less loneliness in the kibbutz, referring perhaps to being in the company of people.

Ruthellen: Yes, it's this sense of being together, and doing together, but I think that we all have examples of how, in order to share, there has to be some distance. And I have a participant who talked about feeling close to people in the kibbutz only once he moved away, for just this reason. That then when he would come back on weekends, he would have things to share, and people there would have things to share, and they could feel that they were talking to each other across some separation of experience.

What both of you have described is the same experience of traveling with somebody for a very long time. If you've experienced exactly the same things for an entire day, by the time you get to sit down for dinner, there really isn't very much to share, because you've done so much together as a single unit, there isn't that difference you can share across. What I find with my participants, though, is that where there is real sharing and intimacy (what we're calling intimacy, in the sense of deep disclosure about oneself, and mutual empathy with the other person, who's also disclosing, not for the purpose of validation, but for the purpose of the joys of sharing and the joys of that kind of connection), people who are kibbutz-raised tend to find people outside of the kibbutz to have these relationships with, if they have them at all. And so it may not be until they have the wherewithal to be outside the kibbutz that it really occurs.

That's why I wonder, in terms of your research, Amia, if maybe it's the result of people still being on the kibbutz, that they haven't really had an opportunity to make outside relationships. Many people will say that once they went to the regional high school, they made a very close friend with someone from another kibbutz, or as soon as they went to the army, they found a real buddy there of some sort, who they really could share with. And then, when they would try to bring this capacity back to the kibbutz, as you said, they really couldn't because the social style in the kibbutz was not one of real disclosure about the self, but rather a being together in a different level of mutuality, companionship. It may also again be in the service of preventing too much exclusivity. There aren't secrets, there isn't anything that sets people apart from the companions of the group.

Ruth: In order to relate to another person exclusively, you have to see that person as unique or outstanding or different from yourself. If we go back to the Freudian perspective, Douvan and Adelson (1966) claimed that adolescent girls have more mutual self-disclosing dialogues because they're trying to clarify mutually the nature of their female genitalia (which is less clear than the nature of male genitalia). The Sullivanian notion is of finding yourself within the similarities, so there has to be some balance of sharing and similarity, on the one hand, and sufficient differences, so that when you're bringing it in, it's not just the merging of experience, but it's really the give and take. . . .

We have a study with Rachel Hertz-Lazarowitz (Sharabany & Hertz-Lazarowitz, 1981) in which we went to kindergartens and first-grade classes, and we had kids sit together and draw on a single sheet of paper, and we chose pairs of friends and nonfriends. One of the findings was that nonfriends shared more and communicated more than friends. It was like married couples not talking and just getting things done. It had the same flavor of things running smoothly—you know the other one, you don't have to make yourself known, it's relatively comfortable. But then what you are missing is really the whole process of finding out new things, because on the one hand, you don't need it, but on the other hand, that may be missing.

Amia: Maybe you need to fight and you need to quarrel. If we really take the marriage metaphor, you need sometimes to fight in order to develop yourself in your relationship, but children in the kibbutz are prohibited from fighting with each other in the peer group, so everything is kind of played down, the emotional side. I wanted to add one thing, that the only two cases in which I have men talking clearly about relationships on the kibbutz and what they need and what they miss is on this dimension, and they are both second-generation men. They speak in exactly the same language about the situation: that they don't have close friends in the kibbutz, but they do have them outside of the kibbutz. Both of them talk about military buddies that belong to other kibbutzim, and they visit each other, and they feel free to expose themselves as human beings totally with someone outside the community, but they say that within the community, it is simply structurally impossible.

Ruth: It's not safe.

Hadas: I have an example of feeling that it's not safe, and actually I did find a trend with Sharabany's Intimacy scale for less trust in same-sex friendships among kibbutzniks, compared to people raised in the city (see Sharabany, 1974, 1994a, 1994b). This woman says,

> When I was growing up, I never had close female friends. I had girlfriends I used to go around with, according to the needs. I didn't feel that there was a girl I felt close enough to that she would not betray me, because here you're friends with everyone, and it's not that you are my friend and not her friend in a small circle. So you are sitting with me, and I'm telling you stuff, and tomorrow you are sitting with another friend, and even without any bad intention, you talk also about this. So there is a problem here, that I can't feel really open, because I can't really trust you with the more important, serious things.

This woman says that when she was away from the kibbutz for a year after high school, that was the first time she learned to open up to another girl. It's interesting that these girls did open up to the boys, to boyfriends, but somehow they felt particularly threatened in close same-sex friendships. That they can't really share, but with a boyfriend, they usually did feel they could share, that he was someone they could trust not to tell other people. Don't you think there is some relation to validation? Because I find that the ones who feel some uniqueness also report that they have a best friend. There is another woman who says that she always had a best friend, and everybody knew that this was her best friend, and she says it was quite unusual actually, because others did have best friends, but they used to switch. She had a best friend for a long time.

Ruth: Did she explain why she was different?

Hadas: Yes, she did see it as something different, and she said, "I'm that kind of person who always needs someone by my side," and that she likes to have a deep relationship.

Ruth: In our adult study with Dana-Engelstein (published in Rabin & Beit-Hallahmi, 1982), kibbutz participants reported that they prefer "many superficial relations" over "few and deep ones."

Amia: But I think it is actually a question of strength rather than dependence. She's strong enough to protect this important relationship, vis-à-vis all the gossip and all the pressure to remain in line all together, all the same. So I think that in the kibbutz, in childhood, it's an achievement to keep a good friend.

Hadas: When I compare this woman to the one who said that she never had a close female friend when she was growing up, the woman who had a best friend was much less vulnerable, she was more secure, she was more spontaneous and less inhibited.

Ruth: So maybe in a circular way, she was able to trust more than other kids did, because confiding or even showing dependence in some ways makes you more vulnerable.

Hadas: In fact, a lot of them said that their parents don't have any close friends, so maybe if they don't have a model of a mother who has a close friend, it's less likely to develop for them, too.

Amia: I think that this is also true of other groups that live in very closed and static settings, that they learn to willingly put up a boundary and to refrain from developing intimate relationships. In my material about prisoners of war, this is really the major conclusion, when they discuss the survival of the group. There were 10 men in one room, which is, of course, even more crowded than the kibbutz, but the peer group of the kibbutz is perhaps similar. The men were grownups, and they had had intimate relationships before, they were capable of intimacy and of deep and profound relationships, but in the prison, they somehow learned to develop a climate of a lot of support and respect for each other, but not to go deeper, and not to reveal emotions. Even instances of emotional exposure were very indirect, such as one man noticing that the other one was crying and joining him quietly, in his walk in the dark courtyard, but never saying anything and never sharing the content of the emotion. It is like an explosive, you have to be careful about what will happen tomorrow when you fight over the line for the shower or when you are really exposing yourself in another way and you have shown your weakness. So I think that this is perhaps an outcome of the lack of ability to move out of the system. When the system is closed, you develop a superficial mutuality with a lot of support, with holding, but not with intimacy.

Ruthellen: That's why I think that it's really complicated to talk about this dimension without just loading it up with a lot of values and judgment here, because we hear this also from training groups, for example, or groups of students. I've had the experience of trying to do a self-study group with my students, and they say, in effect, "Look, if you're trying to push us to be self-revealing, it's going to ruin our closeness and our mutuality."

What they're talking about is a different level of mutuality. In my terms, they're superficially mutual, they are together, they feel very harmonious. When my students come to me for this work, they have already spent a year together, and they've all gotten to know each other, and they're all friendly, and they have parties, and they like each other, and they help each other with homework, and they all get along very well. Then I put them in a self-study group, and the pressure is to go deeper than that, to be more self-disclosing, and they really fight against doing that for fear that it's going to disrupt the relationships, which in fact it does. Their question is, and I suppose it's also my question, is it worth it? They get to a different level of intimacy, but they also pay a price for that.

I think that it's the same kind of thing with your prisoners and also the kibbutzniks: It's not that one level is necessarily better than another. It's deeper perhaps, it's closer. There are also joys in the other kind of mutuality, which I think does prevent people from feeling lonely in the sense that it is usually thought of, that is, without companionship, without someone to at least share activities with.

Ruth: I have an association to this. I think that very often women's friendships, at least partly, are used for talking about the intimate relationship women have with their spouses. Sometimes it is connected with women thinking of the man as less capable of intimacy than women, but I don't think it's the whole story. I think that part of the story is really taking out something from the relationship, being able to observe it from some alternative relationship, from a distance, rather than exploding or taking really intense emotions and clarifying them within the heterosexual relationship. I think that in a way, a self-study group has the potential of erupting in so many ways and not necessarily being resolved in harmony, and healthy solutions could be various. So

Mutuality and Resonance 111

I think that there is something about being constantly in a relationship that doesn't allow you to examine it, and you need to take a step away from the relationship in order to have the perspective on it and to deal with it more, to process it.

Hadas: I just had an association that the term *the communal education* uses the same word as *sharing* in Hebrew, as if the whole kibbutz idea is sharing: You're sharing your property, you're sharing everything, and then there is very little room left for emotional sharing.

Ruthellen: You can only share what's communal, you can't share what's unique—that's the problem these people have. That's the kind of mutuality that's encouraged, that's the idea of taking all the kids on the field trip, rather than asking each kid, what would you uniquely like to do today, and trying to work out something that both people would want to do. That's a collaboration of selves, and that's a completely different kind of sharing. Kibbutz members don't really get to experience that until they have some chance to be away.

One of the things I learned from my participants is that at least among the older ones, they had very few opportunities to do that. Many of the kibbutzim didn't even have telephones, so if members would meet somebody outside, it would be very hard to maintain a relationship, unless they wrote letters or worked very hard at it. It wasn't the kind of thing that you take for granted as we do, you call someone up, or you just get in your car and go visit, or "let's have lunch." It's very hard to do that in this environment, because you were physically so stuck, and then you pay a price in terms of your own environment if you're seeing somebody outside. You have to kind of justify that or have a reason or excuse, or something like that.

Ruth: I think that the boundaries of the kibbutz, the social boundaries, have changed. One reason, which you mentioned, is the telephone, or access to transportation or whatever, but I also think that the whole idea of the volunteers must have been some kind of exposure to the outside world, maybe even in a very invading way, in a threatening way. It's not only that you could now start getting out into the world, but the world has come to your own home, and it is doing all kinds of things, good and bad.

I have the idea—I have no data to go by—that the period when volunteers came from abroad to live and work on the kibbutzim for a time must have had an impact on the nature of close relationships and intimacies. The volunteers provided the option to have friendships that might be intense because of the needs of the volunteers. Also, because the volunteers would come and go, they could give kibbutz members a chance to relate outside of the group. There was quite a contrast between the closed small communities of the kibbutzim before and after the era of the volunteers. I'm just wondering if you have any data in the interviews about what happens in relation to the volunteers, who I think have become an important ingredient in most kibbutzim now.

Amia: I know that both in my material and in Hadas's material, that volunteers provided an opportunity for creating very intense emotional relationships. Many kibbutz members left the kibbutzim with the volunteers, and the problem of Jews and non-Jews has created so much unease that several kibbutzim decided to stop the volunteering. In addition, volunteers were always blamed for all the wrong, the drugs and alcoholism, and so on, but this is not our subject. There is obviously a tendency to create more relationships with somebody who comes from the outside. With all these well-known people around you, as people complain, to see a new face is an exciting relief.

Hadas: Going back to Ruthellen's point that we shouldn't lose sight of the positive side, as well, in the kibbutz, there is the sense that you are never alone, which has both a benefit side and a cost side. The good side is that you're always in company, and there's always someone.

Amia: But I think this is embeddedness, no?

Ruthellen: I think Hadas's point is that if people feel connected to other people, that there's companionship available, that they don't have to stay home all by themselves if they're feeling lonely, that all they have to do is go outside and go to the dining hall or something like that. There's some presumption that people will greet and include each other in some way, so that's something that seems to be taken for granted among kibbutz-raised people, but very much prominent among nonkibbutz-raised people. I think that people who were not on the kibbutz were more likely to put on their charts a tennis partner or the woman I meet at the hairdresser's or something like that, just someone that they interact with, whereas kibbutz people take that much more for granted. There is a loneliness in city life that isn't there on kibbutzim.

10 EMBEDDEDNESS

Amia: If I define embeddedness as belonging to a group, or having your place in a group, I think again that this is an essential feature of the kibbutz life, because it is a very well-defined system, and everybody is part of the system. This is one of the major aspects of kibbutz life: It gives a lot of security, and a feeling of belongingness, and so on, to the people. I think that it is expressed more by people who do not belong and want to join, so a whole chapter on absorptions in my book about Kibbutz Makom, the process of coming in, deals with it again and again.

Kibbutz Makom had several waves of immigrants joining. Each immigrant wave had its own nationality, and when people came in, they had their own customs and so on, and each group looked at the former one as "the cream of the earth," which they wanted to join. The importance of joining in, and being accepted, is expressed in many very moving stories, especially for instance, those of the Polish women. When the Polish women came, the kibbutz consisted of two ethnic groups: the Israeli-born and the German-born, and the Polish were looked down upon. They come from this perspective, looking at the songs that the Israelis sing and the impolite way that they communicate and talk to each other, the loudness, the filth in the dining room.

Everything is turned into a positive thing, because they want to belong. To belong means to lose weight and to grow taller, which you cannot do, but to speak Hebrew like a native, and to eat noisily and impolitely, and other things.

The way that people speak about this 50 years later shows you that all they wanted was to belong, to be identified as a member of the group. The whole concept of membership, of course, is defined on the kibbutz in a technical way: to be a "candidate" for a year or two, then to be elected and accepted as a member, and to maintain your membership, or to leave. So all this is very strong.

Another manifestation of this embeddedness is the holidays in the kibbutzim. This was expressed when I asked people about what things they miss in the kibbutz life, when they left it, or spontaneously with the stories about the wonderful nights of a holiday celebration on the kibbutz, that there is nothing like it. When I asked what they felt, the answer was, "I felt one of the collective. I felt that the kibbutz is a community, that each one is important, that I am important. Singing together, the music, spending the time together, the togetherness."

Therefore, I think that embeddedness in the kibbutz is really something very concrete, and its major trend is positive. People talk about being part of a group as a very positive thing, but again, you'll find a few who say that it's too much, that it creates pressure, that it goes against individuation as a separate person, as we discussed a lot in the validation section.

Ruth: Just as we talked about ideology as some kind of a message or a representation of the community, I think that this embeddedness, or oneness, is also something that you find outside of the kibbutz. For example, it can be expressed as longing for a family holiday, or myths of what holidays are for people, such as the fantasy that it is the time the whole family is together and happy.

Amia: But here it is not a fantasy, it's reality, and it has not been burned out by time, as ideology has. Ideology has gone through a terrible decline, and people are questioning it, finding the need for change, and there is a lot of struggle and conflict around this. Embeddedness is something that succeeded in the kibbutz, and people really feel that this is a concept that they are not ambivalent about. It's not a fantasy. I think that it is there.

Ruthellen: Well, the people experience this, what Buber calls the "being bound up together," being connected in some very deep way to this culture which is much larger than the self. I think the notion is even different from ideology, in the sense that one is tied to some stream of something that is larger than the self, that it can't be represented by an individual but has to be embodied in a group somehow, and that one has a place in this ongoing march of history. So that whether one leaves the kibbutz or doesn't, if you were raised on the kibbutz, the notion of belonging becomes very charged with a tremendous feeling, because not to belong means to be completely left out and alienated from the society. It's what really holds people in, and what people feel nostalgic for if they leave.

It's hard to know whether it exists in a kind of independent reality. Certainly, it's real in the sense that people experience it as a very strong draw. People feel it in patriotism also, in celebrating Independence Day, when singing the national anthem, or on Jewish holidays, the sense of connection to something that is larger, but in the kibbutz, it's very concrete, it's part of this particular place and our way of doing things.

Buber (1965) says that there is a kind of belonging, as he says "they belong together in a way that is fundamentally different from every possible belonging together with someone outside the group" (pp. 72-73). People seem to talk about it as my kibbutz, that is, my group, and a feeling that this particular kibbutz is different from any other kibbutz. You don't hear that with cities. People will say, "I like my city better than your city," but . . .

Ruth: It's like family.

Ruthellen: In the cultural family sense, in the genealogy, the roots.

Ruth: It's kind of an extended family type of relatedness, and I do think that it's good that you are placing both ends of the continuum here, because I think it does have a strong presence, the whole embeddedness, or the sense of belonging, yet I do believe in individual differences, and in ambivalence, and in different positions relating to it. Somehow I can't recall the name of the writer, but I do remember stories from the literature about how estranged you can feel when everyone is celebrating and you don't feel part of it. How painful it is, and maybe it's not even as painful when you work on holidays, and you don't have your family to celebrate with. Here you are out of the whole community, if you don't connect on these levels. So I feel that as long as we keep it as a dimension on which people are each finding their niche and their variation, I would feel more comfortable than only seeing it as the positive pole of the unifying aspect.

Hadas: So if you don't feel embedded, it's very painful.

Ruthellen: If you don't feel embedded enough, if you get too far in the alienation direction.

Hadas: Another aspect is the sense of lack of opportunities to change your interpersonal relationships and social network within a very static social situation in the kibbutz. For example,

> In the kibbutz, it was clear to me already in advance what the opportunities were outside of my room. Who is out there and what I can do with them, and what kind of relationship I can expect to have with them if I go out of my room and relate to them. There was nothing there that interested me as a meaningful relation, because I knew that beyond what I had already, I wouldn't be able to find it there. In the city, at least there is always the feeling that the opportunities are open, that maybe now I don't know that many people, but soon I will, that potential, and it doesn't even matter if it actually happens or not, but there is a feeling of an open situation, a dynamic one, not a static situation, that is actually determined ahead of time, and that I can't change it, and it isn't really in my hands.

Ruth: This is an embeddedness that you feel ambivalent about.

Ruthellen: Yes, that you're questioning, you're wondering about how it could be different. I'm doing another paper on the adolescent crisis as the possible split between attachment and embeddedness. People have talked about adolescence as being a time when adolescents detach from parents, but that is clearly not what they do—the research shows that that is not what is happening. The question is how can psychologists confuse that so much?

I think that what is actually happening is that adolescents are beginning to consider new contexts for embeddedness but not new attachments. Adolescents want to maintain their sense of attachment to parents, but they are trying to think about how to do that in perhaps a different context of embeddedness. That is, can I join this other set of values, or way of living, or group, or something like that, and still stay connected to my parents? This may be what some of the tension is about, in the adolescent-parent struggle, and everybody is mixed up about those two dimensions. The parents are afraid that if the adolescent goes off into this new belief system, they will lose their child, the attachment is going to be broken, when it's really just a new context that the person wants.

Ruth: Yes, but you have just touched on one of the problems that could exist with kibbutz embeddedness, which is its totality—just as much as this is its strength. Within the kibbutz, you can be embedded and belong, but there are not enough networks and niches so that you can go from one to another and still be within the kibbutz.

Amia: I want to give you an example from a woman who died of cancer about 3 weeks after this interview. She was taken back to the kibbutz to improve her quality of life before her death, and she was fully aware of the situation. People said to me, "Go interview her very fast, because it's the last chance." I was hesitant, and I thought I'll find this sickly woman (she was younger than me; she was about 40), but I found such a brave woman, and I think that she got some wisdom from her approaching end. She says,

> The idea of a community is a central principle in our kibbutz. A community is made up of many elements. If some are eliminated, the whole will become unbalanced. Although it's true that not everybody wants to be a teacher, our local school provides jobs for many people, not only in teaching, but in workshop, construction, many things that are interdependent.

So she goes on speaking about the group as functioning together, and it's very much like what you said about Buber. One of the nicest examples she gives me of the ways in which this is a community, what makes it unique, is the following:

> Many of us study in various programs, or at the Open University. We also have ongoing classes here. Last year, we added a new program that studies the history and philosophy of the labor movement in Israel. It was initiated during the winter, twice a

week at 5:30 in the morning. I would be getting up at 4:30, when it was still completely dark, putting on the light. I used to see my mother, who is 70 now, also turning on the light in her room to get ready for our class. Before sunrise, this group would gather in the school building together with some teachers we had invited for this purpose. All of us were pretty advanced in years—most of us were parents or grandparents—and we'd crowd into our children's classroom for an early morning lesson. At the beginning, we were laughed at, losing sleep to study A. D. Gordon, but soon they stopped laughing. Frequently, our children, who start their school day at 6:30, would come to class and see us still absorbed in our studies. Patiently they waited at the doorstop for their parents and grandparents to leave their classroom, and then they take their seats, as we leave school for our day's work.

I think that this is the continuity you are speaking about.

It is just an example, but there is so much meaning in this single act of daybreak study of the labor movement ideology in our children's classroom. I can't even start to unearth it all. We all live and study here together.

So this is embeddedness when it works, but for some people it doesn't.

Ruth: I really was wondering how much parents delegated their connections with their children at some level to educators, to metaplot, and how much they had input into their children's lives beyond the approved time slot. What I see in that description she gave is some level of connection.

Amia: This is embeddedness. It's not just containing on the surface, it's the interrelationship between all the elements. I think that this is a beautiful description.

Ruth: That it does happen.

Amia: On the good kibbutzim. At the time, they were not too big, and they were pretty secure economically, and they felt like a successful human experiment. I think it was much more prevalent, more than today. It was not so unusual. My interviewee had a very good way of describing it, by using this metaphor of the rotation, parts of the population using the same little chairs and benches to study different subjects.

Hadas: This refers to the multigenerational aspect of kibbutz life. With the young people, it seems that some really appreciate it and see it as an opportunity to be close to people that they can learn from. They have this project where students help old people in the kibbutz clean their apartments, and some interviewees spoke about it as a welcomed opportunity to interact with old people. Others really reject the opportunities and feel suffocated.

Amia: Maybe you need to be older to appreciate this. Even to be able to observe it, to discriminate this from other experiences.

Ruthellen: I think that when embeddedness is really operative, it disappears completely, even more so than holding. One feels so much a part of whatever one is a part of that you almost don't notice it. It's your place, it's your group, it's your country, it's your whatever it is, and it's simply not questioned, it's just a part of the terrain.

Ruth: I think maybe another aspect—I'm not sure, but maybe it's related—is the whole relation between your work and your family. In the United States, there were periods when many people talked about the "compartmentalization" of the adult world, of the work world, the disconnection. Your example reminded me that a kid in the kibbutz could have a better chance of seeing his parents at work, his parents' colleague relationships, his parents in other contexts. On this level of what you are calling embeddedness, there is this interdependence and crossing of boundaries, which can make you more familiar with the world of your parents or your grandparents, or whatever, in a way that you don't feel in other contexts.

Again, you can take it for granted, that you know at a certain time of the day, you can find your mother exactly there, or your father there. However, I think that the price is that children saw their parents less, maybe, in their pajamas and quarreling, or how they look in the middle of the night when something happens, or just daily life. So some intimacy is missing.

Ruthellen: And from an early age, people are given a place. It's not like American society, where one doesn't get a place until after graduation from college. From an early age, everyone contributes, everyone has their job, their expectations, and so on. It's a very highly socialized environment and therefore very difficult to break away from. That's why the leavers seem to struggle so much and look for another community to embed in, which is the community of the leavers. Very often, they'll find other former kibbutzniks, to try to find a new group like that.

Ruth: One of my students used the expression, that in New York, there is a community of "kibbutz survivors." They carry this feeling of having a mutual and common experience, looking for this, and re-creating communal life in some sense. She says the amount of embeddedness and support that goes on there is something that they have in common, and of course, paradoxically, they left one context of embeddedness to re-create another one that they are familiar with.

Ruthellen: But it's that need to belong, to feel that one is part of the group, or other people sharing the same experiences. . . . There are others who very much belong. The ones who are still in the kibbutzim feel a very strong sense of continuing connection, of having their place. Some of them are people who were lost without that.

One of the life stories I reported was a man who came as a child and was the son of immigrants. The whole goal of his life was to try to belong. He just desperately wanted to belong, and what he's done through his life is whatever he could do to be part of this. And he's had all these children, and he populated the kibbutz, and he's become the manager, and so on. He wanted a place. He did not want to feel like an outsider anymore.

I think it's like validation in the sense that where people feel most themselves very much affects their history. Those who felt outside as children seem to be those who most wanted to dedicate their life to belonging. Those who had a smooth course seem to feel more options, although there are those who didn't belong, and they just want to get out. Maybe it's that people who didn't belong are just more sensitized to finding somewhere they can belong, if not the kibbutz, then elsewhere.

Amia: You must remember that if you talk about the kibbutz in the context of Israel, a lot of these people are immigrants, or immigrants' children. The mentality of cultural transition, questions about where you belong and what is your language and which songs you can sing with the group and so on, are a real issue for many of these people.

Ruthellen: It's a very important aspect of connection. I think that in psychology, we just don't talk about that much. It somehow falls between the cracks. We take it for granted or something. I think this is a terribly important way in which people orient themselves to others, and it's very, very basic.

Amia: In my Gestalt groups, it comes up from time to time with new immigrants, or people on a transitional basis here, overseas students, the difficulty of belonging when you come from another culture. The difficulty of writing, for example. I remember the first time I realized the difficulty for somebody who wants to be a poet, and her language is Hungarian, so then she turned to English, and then to Hebrew. The dilemmas of what language she's writing in, and what language her metaphors come from. It's really a tremendous task to become embedded, and I think language is very central here.

Ruthellen: It's the first act of embeddedness that we make, which is to try to make the same sounds as the people around us, rather than our own sounds. By learning that, we join the culture.

Hadas: Think about the words that you use in a kibbutz, so if you are a kibbutz member you are referred to as a *chaver*, meaning you're a comrade/friend. It seems that in the kibbutz there is a great emphasis on belonging and being part of the kibbutz.

Ruthellen: There is always a tradeoff between the individual and the group.

Amia: Collectivity can take priority over the individual, or the large group takes priority over the small group.

11 TENDING (CARE)

Ruth: My association to tending has to do with parenting, which is definitely not the only perspective of tending, because it can be on all levels, but I'm looking for an excuse to talk about the place of women and their relationships in the kibbutz, and I thought this would be a nice door to smuggle it in through. I'm very puzzled by the whole shift in sex roles of women in the kibbutz, in which recently they are reclaiming a lot of their traditional jobs.

I think women must have been missing this whole experience of taking care of, of being tender toward, and missing this intimate level. I think that part of delegating the role of raising your children to other people, part of the constraints on intimacy that we saw, must have been badly missed by women—maybe by others, too, but we know that women are more sensitive to this area. I think that part of moving into family sleeping arrangements is reclaiming the part of taking care and the tenderness that can be more intimate and personal when it's not communal and collective and public. Bettelheim (1969) talks about it, that women used to sit and nurse in a group, which probably, on the one hand, supported them as a net of some kind but, on the other hand, robbed them of their intimate or very personal connection to their baby.

Hadas: Yet they were taking care of everybody else's children.

Ruth: Yes, and they were getting all the service jobs, which are really taking care of education.

Amia: But if they needed to express tenderness, they should have been happy in these jobs, but they were miserable. If I followed your argument, you said that they needed to find a place to show their tenderness, and they could do that toward the children they took care of as metapelet. Usually, this is not what happened.

Ruth: Yes, but that's not intimate. I think there is this Marxist term of alienation, which says that as soon as you are not cooking for yourself, and not cleaning for yourself, and not washing your own clothing, and you are delegating so many chores that have to be very close to your physical self, then at some level, you are creating a distance. I think that in a similar way, taking care of other children is one step removed from your very physical needs and self and whatever. I think on a more general level, that women have always been more connected to this aspect, which unfortunately involved doing lower status things. But I think that what women won by this is that they were always closer to what they felt and to their bodies, much more than men are to theirs.

Amia: I think that I have another answer to the question . . . why weren't they satisfied? First of all, let us agree on the facts, that taking care of other children as a metapelet, for most of the women I interviewed, was a terribly frustrating and difficult job, with a huge amount of burnout.

Ruthellen: I have a couple of participants who did put children that they took care of on their relational chart.

Amia: Maybe retrospectively, and maybe today it's not so hard. I'm talking about my data. They all compare and say that in the past, the groups were larger and the physical conditions were harder. One woman was isolated with a group of four tiny children for the whole day. Today, they usually have two metaplot with a larger group of six children, so they can go out and breathe and have a cigarette or coffee. They had a very difficult time on the job, and I think it did not satisfy their need for tending, partly because the job was—you said alienation—but the job was defined with so many rules and regulations about what you should do. It was not what you felt like doing.

This woman Na'ama speaks about her early times as a metapelet in the kibbutz. I quoted her before, about her own daughter, how she felt she was frustrating, even neglecting, her daughter, but that this is what she should do. As a metapelet, she said it was the same:

> It was a horrible time for me. Conditions at work were terrible. We didn't realize that we could take life a bit easier. One metapelet worked with a class of 20 preschool children. Today this same class would have three metaplot and a teacher. It's true that we were short of people, but the real reason for functioning this way was that we simply thought that this was normal. The housing—it was the same houses in which we have 11 or 12 babies today, we used to keep 24 babies, 6 in a room, with six mothers spending half the day in this tiny room breast-feeding their babies. Nobody used formula then. We thought that this was the right way. Our methods of child-rearing were simply ascetic, bathing children in cold water the year round, for instance, because we thought it was healthy and it would immunize the children. How they suffered, the poor things. They hated to take a shower as if it were the worst thing in the world.
>
> Feeding, as well. You remember the horrible stories about how a child had to eat whatever was put on his plate, whatever was cooked that day in the kitchen. We sat with them and made them eat, and if they refused to eat they were given the same plate again at the next meal. At night, they slept on wooden boards, which were considered healthy for their posture.
>
> Today I feel as if I'm talking about medieval ages. I'm not normally a strict person, (and it's true, she's not, far from it), so the whole time that I was raising children this way, it was out of a sense of duty. For me, it was a long ongoing nightmare. I loved the children, and I used to try to compensate for the strictness with games and stories, and by showing my love. I really felt we ought to change the system somehow, but I didn't know how, nor did my friends.

So these are the earlier times, and they're not the earliest. It was impossible to be tender, tenderness had no place.

Ruthellen: There was no place for tending in the sense that we're thinking of, what we associate with tenderness, that is, feeling cooey and harmonious and close, but this was an aspect of her tending in the sense that she was using ideology as a form of care. This gets into the whole issue about care being difficult. If people were not as confused about care as they are, then this kind of stuff wouldn't happen. Because people don't really know how to care for other people, ideologies like this can come in and say, "This is what's good for children." Since mothers, or caretakers, are confused about that, they'll say "Oh, if this is what the experts say, that this is the right way to raise a good kid, then who am I to say that this would really be better for them?"

You can look at the history of childhood in these terms all the way along, that mothers are always sold these ideas, and they adopt them out of a wish to care for the children. They want so much to be perfect and to do right by their children that they feel guilty if they would do something else. They're afraid they'll spoil the child, or kill his posture, and so on. That continues. When we look back 50 years from now at our child-raising methods today, the next generation is going to say the same thing: "Can you believe that this is what they did?" Our theories make lots of sense now, out of a wish to care.

Ruth: Another point that I think we can make on the aspect of tending is what you mentioned about the elderly. Someone in my seminar read a study comparing taking care of elderly people in the kibbutz and in the United States. Although the comparison is really too confounded to say anything, I'll mention it anyway. What they were comparing was the aspect of adjustment and health, being kept out of an institution when you have more personal care versus professional care. They chose the kibbutz because potentially they thought this could be a place where there is more personal care.

They found, within the kibbutz, a difference between members who joined later with their parents, so that the elderly were parents, where the children were involved directly in their care, as opposed to elderly members whose kibbutz-raised children seemed to delegate their parents' care to the kibbutz. In general, they did find that in the kibbutz, the conditions of the elderly are, of course, much better than in some alienated urban place, but I think the confounded aspect is the extent to which the kibbutz people were able to care for their own parents. That I'm not clear about.

I think it is still an open question for me, does the kibbutz prepare you to care personally? Which is where I connect this to being tender, and in my mind, if as a child, your parents weren't the immediate, primary source of comfort that they could have been, then I don't think you would be able, as a grownup, to care for your own parents in the connected, primary, warm, and close way, because I think you would be applying a similar perspective of independence, or of not showing emotions, or of coping, of separateness, or whatever.

Amia: I think that the whole kibbutz notion about taking care of the elderly as well as sick people is very technical and very professionally oriented. They create little systems like a small nursing home, or a small hospital, with people who work there around the clock. The family is relieved of taking care of a member who is sick or old and replaced by the system. When I discussed this with the person who was at that time the head of the health committee, she said to me,

> What do you expect? We cannot rely on the normal things to happen. That is too dangerous. We have to supply everything around the clock all day, and if the family can chip in, that's wonderful, but you cannot rely on the family.

For instance, when a person from the kibbutz goes to the hospital, the health committee will go to members and say, "Do you know that so-and-so is in the hospital? Go and visit him." Everything is organized, so gradually the spontaneous caretaking is being reduced to a very small fraction of life. In order to be such a welfare community, everything is under control, an organization, part of the duties, so the spontaneous gentleness and relational tending is less and less pronounced. Funerals, for instance: You have to call people and say, "Please make an effort to come."

Ruthellen: Really?

Ruth: Yes, that's the story about larger kibbutzim. They say there could be a funeral at one end and some other happening at the other end of the kibbutz. It was explained to me as part of the size of the kibbutz, but maybe it's not only that. It's part of anti-embeddedness or differentiation.

Amia: I say that it's a lack of tenderness, very little spontaneous care, but maybe it's my hunch.

Hadas: There is a sense, however, that older people on the kibbutz, even if their sons and daughters don't physically take care of them, they feel more secure if their children are on the kibbutz. They feel very helpless, and that they have very little influence, if they're aging on the kibbutz without having their sons and daughters there.

Ruthellen: My participants—and I may have a very skewed sample—but all of my older participants feel a very strong responsibility for taking care of aging parents, and they seem to work very hard at that. With how much love or affection, I don't know, but they actually do it. The ones who are off the kibbutz go and visit periodically, especially when their mothers are there. They don't at all seem to be leaving the care for mother just to the kibbutz. They have a real sense of responsibility, guilt if they don't visit often enough, and a sense of real involvement.

One of the early things that I find among my participants, which I found very interesting, was the degree to which people felt responsible as children for younger siblings. As though this was the laboratory for learning about care. Almost because the parents weren't there so much of the time. If they were all in the children's house, the older siblings would take it on themselves to look out for the younger ones. Many of them felt very parental toward these younger ones. They would give them advice, they'd look after them, just kind of keep an eye out, and back at home they would play with them and teach them and become kind of miniparents in a way. Often these relationships were maintained, with ups and downs, moving apart and getting back together, but the sibling relationship seemed to be very intense in this caretaking way. What that seemed to lead to, especially for the men, was a real orientation to care for their children.

Amia: That's a completely different generation then.

Ruthellen: The ages are quite varied. In both samples, those still on the kibbutz, and not on the kibbutz, ranged in age from 28 to about 50. So it spans both generations.

Amia: But this is a trend in the whole society in Israel, of men becoming more involved in child care. I found a quotation about spontaneity from a social secretary, a man. He says,

We are an institutionalized society. The more formally organized we are, to meet every individual need, the less spontaneously we express solidarity in our lives. We are a big community, no longer an extended family, and we can't rely on spontaneous support in cases of private crisis or hardship, so we organize the support through functionaries and committees, and this in turn reduces the need for spontaneous involvement even more. People who live here know that somebody else will take care of the unpleasant business, and after a while, they cease to be interested in their roles as individual contributors.

He brings several examples about funerals, and so on.

Take for example our care for drafted soldiers or hospitalized members. We don't rely on the family or close friends to visit and maintain contact with the individual. We appoint special committees to regulate these things. These appointed people serve as a collective superego, one might say, thus freeing the individual members of their own moral responsibilities. Often we forget to visit our hospitalized friends, unless someone from the health committee has put a note in your box, and supplied the transportation. That's not good, I know, yet I prefer this situation to a system which relies on spontaneity, which might or might not exist when it's needed.

And he goes on,

Look, we are real life people with real life needs that must be dealt with. It's not a lark, a youth movement, or a summer camp. We have people with all sorts of serious problems, many old and sick people, people who need welfare. It's not a game any more.

As if spontaneous tenderness and caring for others is not enough, and so it needs regulation. I think that this is a very observant remark, which you don't hear frequently. What has happened as an outcome of the kibbutz common education, and all the other beautiful institutions, is that they have somehow emptied the more natural flow of interrelationships. It is similar to what we said about intimate friendships, a similar outcome.

Ruth: We are comparing spontaneous care by individuals, mostly family members, with organized care by the kibbutz. It may be that the kibbutz has succeeded much more than other societies in providing and regulating care for children and particularly for the elderly. It is possible that compared to the very committed care of a family member or a friend, the kibbutz seems to provide impoverished institutional care. However, compared to the less enthusiastic or less capable spontaneous care that many family members and friends provide in cities, the kibbutz has done wonders for its elderly. Making friends and relatives more "relaxed" about their involvement does carry the same danger we have been talking about: less closeness for better as well as for worse.

Amia: Yes, but I think that now the trend is going up again, to have more personal care among people who care about each other, and not because it is a job. At first, you see it in the family, a sick child being treated by his or her mother. It will always be the parent who takes the child to the hospital or to the doctor, or has the deepest concern about the child, which was not the practice before. I believe that it will catch on in other relationships, maybe with the elderly, as well, with the relaxation of the collective and the coming back of the individual into the kibbutz. It may encourage more of the spontaneous and normal caregiving functions among people, which will not be institutionalized so much, as the secretary said.

Ruth: Amia, in your example, incidentally or not, you mentioned the family together with the deeper, the personal, and I really wonder about that, from a general perspective. Why is it that the family is such a center, a center of care, of connectedness, why is it? Is it because of the biological link? Because we talked about friendships, and we talked about intimacy, yet when you looked for an example or a synonym for a deep caring, a personal caring, the term family came up. It could be just that you are describing reality, but this is something, you know the term "just friends," always haunts me, especially on kibbutzim. Why is it?

Ruthellen: There are still a lot of examples in my data. I don't know if it's any more or less so on the kibbutz, but there are a lot of examples of feeling caring and tender toward friends, and connecting to people around being needed. People put friends on the diagram, "because a friend was going through a hard time and really needed me at this point, and therefore I was spending a lot of time and energy caring for my friend." But it's true, why the family? It really goes back to your question: Why does it feel better to care for your own infant than to care for somebody else's infant?

I think this is really where tending and attachment start meeting each other. It's something about the sense of caring for someone with whom I will have a continuous relationship, and it's something about merging those experiences. People did talk about relationships they had in which they were very giving and caring, and all that was very important to them, but where it was a relationship that was time-limited, it seemed to have less meaning over the whole life span. It may have had a lot of meaning, maybe in the validation direction, as in "I took care of this person, I helped them after their accident," or "I kept them from committing suicide," or whatever it was, and "I learned that I really am a very giving person, and that I could really go into a helping profession." So it might be that the care then would reverberate on the validation dimension.

But what we hear seems to be that marriage and care and attachment lead to a very intense loving kind of persistence that tends to be centered more on the family. I don't hear about the institutional things but, of course, I'm not asking about that. I'm asking people about important people.

Amia: I don't ask either, I give them a lot of freedom about what they want to bring up. If this person is the social secretary, then he has the perspective of the social needs of the community. But I think that he did not exaggerate too much, because he gave many examples.

To your question, Ruth—it's really a very good question—I think that the "stream of life" is going from a mother or a father, a mother caring for the child, and then eventually the child caring for elderly parents. This is really the life cycle, essentially. Around it, you have a lot of other people caring for each other, but this is the major continuous human cycle.

I had many moving discussions about this dying woman, Ziva. She was such a beloved member of the group, and everyone was aware of the terminal state of her cancer, and that was why they brought her back to the kibbutz to die. Several people talked to me about caring for Ziva, and coming to stay with her, and wanting to make her life as easy as possible. Not all were members of her family. One was a sister-in-law, which is not really close family. She was a single woman. She explained to me—although I didn't ask why she never married—she said that for years, she was taking care of her brother's family because his wife was so sick and going in and out of hospitals.

Another woman who mentioned caring for Ziva (it's only women) is Tikva, a writer. I have written about her, an elderly woman writer who is rather famous in Israel, who lives in this kibbutz. She writes all day, she goes to eat in the dining room when she feels like it, nobody gives her any jobs, but she's still a member there, considered eccentric, an individualist. By the way, Tikva lost her son in the war, which added more status to her, so no one bothers her. She told me that voluntarily—nobody asked her—she used to stay nights with Ziva at her bedside, and when Ziva couldn't sleep, they would study together and they would talk, and they would tell each other about their lives, although she was much older than Ziva, and they were not friends before.

So there are instances of caring outside the family, but if Tikva had not done that, the kibbutz would have made sure that somebody was there with Ziva during her bad nights, and it would never be left to her family, or neglected and fall between the different authorities.

Ruthellen: It was very hard for me, being an outsider, to really discriminate how much of this was a function of the kibbutz and how much is Israeli society, as I said before. I think Israeli society is a more care-oriented society, in general, so I don't know if I really hear a difference between the kibbutz-raised and nonkibbutz-raised Israelis. In both groups, there seems to be a real commitment, at least to seeing oneself as a person who does offer care, and to maintaining relationships, pretty much at all points of life, that at least feel mutually caring. It seems that most people try to have at least somebody that they feel they are caring for, if it's not friends, then it may be students, or it may be the children in the children's house, or something like that, but people tend to see themselves as caring people.

Amia: The Orthodox Jews do it as a *mitzvah*, and the Sephardis are very much oriented toward really helping. It's really Jewish, I think.

Ruthellen: It's in Christian theology too, but it doesn't come out as much.

Amia: It comes out at Christmas. Then you have to do some good deeds.

Ruthellen: It's less in the community. I don't know, that may not be a fair generalization.

Hadas: The only example of tending that I had was of a single woman who was about 29, and she got a lot of fulfillment from being caring in her role as metapelet in the kibbutz, and feeling that although she didn't have her own children, she had all these other children whom she was very important to, and she gave them a lot, and she got a lot of respect from the community, the parents appreciated her and what she did for the children.

Amia: I think that if I remember her case, for her this was part of embeddedness, more than the caring sense. She didn't go into the emotional part. She said, "Everybody greets me on the path because I am the metapelet of their children." So I don't know.

Ruth: Your point about the Israeli society in general is very important, and I don't think we can yet exactly identify what it is in Israeli society. Maybe it is still less alienated than, let's say, the urban American one. There is much more familialism, for better and worse. Nepotism is walking free on the streets here, which is not such a legitimate process in other places. We call it *protectsia*, using connections, especially family connections, to get places. When you meet new immigrants who are not your relations, if you really care about them, then you start making your friends work for them, start finding connections. It's not such a clearly illegitimate process, but it is very personalized, it's just there. It's working your way through personal connections, and you mobilize in this direction. It is in a way like networking.

Hadas: It's funny, because it's what the *yordim* (Israelis who left Israel) do abroad: They look after each other. You help another Israeli. If he doesn't have a green card, you give him a job.

Ruth: This was part of the success of the Jewish immigrants to the United States and the Orientals. If you have just one member of your family there, then you already have your foot in the door. I don't know exactly. There are ethnic elements to it, I'm sure.

Ruthellen: In a sense, it's the relationship between caring and embeddedness, in the sense that this is a club, and so everybody who comes here joins the club, and therefore everyone has to take care of the members. It's a small enough club, and because you want to keep members in the club, you have to be nice to all of the members. So there is a real ethic, you protect the society by that. In order to preserve the culture, in order to preserve the embeddedness that is important to everybody, you have to take care of the new members, or else they might leave.

Ruth: It's not really so personalized. In a sense, it's like the kibbutz. It's not that you are doing it only for someone who deserves it, or is a good person. You do it because of the embeddedness. So just because someone is Israeli, you are supposed to give information and to help them.

Hadas: I guess this could bring us to say that our whole discussion about relatedness in the kibbutz should be seen in the Israeli context.

Ruthellen: I think that all the relational dimensions take place within the context of embeddedness. So we're just moving embeddedness one step further, saying that it's all within the embeddedness of Israeli culture, a particular soil in which the kibbutz could grow, which then spawns all of these other phenomena that we're seeing. But you can't ever understand the effects of relatedness outside of the culture that it grows in. If you try to have a kibbutz in Japan, for example, the phenomenon would be completely different.

12 REFLECTIONS ON THE DISCOURSE

HADAS WISEMAN

In reflecting back on the process of the discourse for me, let me first begin with my expectations. In other words, what was my fantasy of what would happen during the discourse, in light of the goals we had? In fact, the goals of the discourse were not explicated ahead of time in a very narrow manner. Doing this was more an idea that intuitively seemed right. I felt it would be exciting and innovative. It seemed like it would serve a need I had with respect to the research I was doing on the kibbutz. How was the mode of the discourse different from other more traditional modes?

One example of a traditional mode is that of a paper presentation in a conference. For a conference, you prepare a paper, usually referring to a specific study you undertook. You try to make a convincing case for your research question, your method, and then you present your results and briefly discuss your findings, including perhaps not only the answers to the question you posed, but also suggesting further

---

AUTHORS' NOTE: These reflections were written by each participant six years after the 1990 discourse recorded in this book.

questions. If you are lucky, you get a few interesting questions from the audience. In some cases perhaps, you are part of a panel of researchers who share your topic of study or methods, and some stimulating exchange goes on. However, most often there is no real time "to talk." Usually, this kind of dialogue or discourse, which I am usually thirsty for, takes place during coffee breaks. After the coffee break, I might even write down an idea or two to remember what was "presented" and discussed during this "time off."

In what way was this discourse different? First, I had prior knowledge and familiarity with the participants' own work on the kibbutz. For me in particular, it was exciting to have this kind of discourse with the other three participants. I knew their separate voices on this topic. My interest in studying individuation and relatedness in the kibbutz was stimulated by Amia's *Kibbutz Makom* (Lieblich, 1981), which I read in Canada during my graduate studies, while I was considering and planning what to study for a postdoctoral Lady Davis Fellowship. The study I eventually conducted a year later in Israel included questionnaires (using Sharabany's Intimacy Scale) and also intensive personal interviews with 50 kibbutz-born young adults. After completing the study, I met Ruthellen Josselson in Jerusalem and was exposed to her ideas on relatedness, which she wrote down in *The Space Between Us* (Josselson, 1992). I was excited to have the opportunity to meet with her and Amia to exchange ideas on her book and her interviews. In the middle of the year, I moved to the University of Haifa and traveled to Jerusalem to continue our meetings. Ruth Sharabany was also interested in Ruthellen's work and how it might shed light on issues that she had studied for almost 20 years.

The idea of putting these women in one room and testing out ideas on relatedness in the kibbutz seemed to me like a rare opportunity. I was truly curious to hear what each had to say. Preparing for the discourse, I went back to my own raw data, particularly the interview data, to pull out examples of expressions of each dimension. This post hoc process presents an interesting hybrid between a theory-based research approach and a discovery-based research approach. As my interview data were collected before I became acquainted with the relatedness dimensions, the raw data are free of preconceived bias toward Josselson's model, and in this sense, they could be viewed as discovery-oriented and exploratory. However, referring to the data according to the dimensions post hoc is theory-based, in that we applied Josselson's category system rather than making an attempt to let the category system emerge through an exploratory process, as is done when applying a grounded theory approach (see Strauss & Corbin, 1990).

In other words, the themes of relatedness were, so to speak, dictated by the eight dimensions, and the issue in question became the extent to which these themes were apparent in the data. The extent to which there seemed to be a good fit between the data and the eight dimensions would not only shed new light on certain aspects of relatedness in the kibbutz that have not been clearly articulated beforehand, but it would also be a way to get a better understanding of the meaning of each dimension. This latter point was among the benefits of the discourse. It enabled an open discussion of the meaning that each of us gave to each of the relatedness dimensions. Thus, the discourse on each dimension provided each participant with a unique opportunity to test out her interpretations of each dimension in the context of studies and data on relatedness in the kibbutz.

The use of narrative accounts within the discourse was in my opinion one of the assets of our method. The richness of the stories people tell, one aspect of this richness being the multiplicity of implications and potential interpretations (Baumeister & Newman, 1994), was to some extent retained by referring to quotations from interviewees, consisting of their own words for telling the story of interpersonal life in the kibbutz. Moreover, the narrative mode seems most appropriate to the study of the kibbutz, as it is context-sensitive rather than free of context.

Studying the area of relatedness in the kibbutz seems to particularly require a context-sensitive methodology. Concepts such as holding and mutuality may have a different meaning within the context of the kibbutz than in the context of the city. The narrative mode seems essential in order to arrive at context-sensitive meanings of the different aspects of relatedness in the kibbutz. Referring to the distinction between narrative thinking and paradigmatic thinking, Baumeister and Newman (1994) assert the following:

> Rich accounts can encompass many features, and so narratives are more flexible and can accommodate more inconsistencies than paradigmatic thinking. . . . The narrative mode is well-suited for reinterpreting and accommodating inconsistent information, as well as for helping people think about situations that involve conflicts or contradictions. (p. 679)

In considering studies on the kibbutz, it is exactly this kind of flexibility which is much needed.

In reflecting on the discourse as methodology, questions may arise with regard to the issues of reliability and validity. The relatively more straightforward issue of reliability can be considered both in terms of consistency and replicability. One could speculate that if the four of us would repeat this process, it would lead for the most part to similar "results" (consistent with the combination of our data, our personalities, and the dynamics of the group process). That is, we would have arrived at some similar aspects; yet, there is the possibility that some aspects or nuances would be different. However, on the whole, the method itself of the discourse could be replicated. What about the more complex issue of validity? To answer this question, I found that the ideas put forward by Mishler (1990) in his article on "Validation in Inquiry-Guided Research" could serve as an important reference point. Mishler reformulates validation as a process through which a community of researchers evaluates the "trustworthiness" of a particular study as the basis for their own work. His argument is as follows:

> Focusing on trustworthiness rather than truth displaces validation from its traditional location in a presumably objective, nonreactive, and neutral reality and moves it to the social world—a world constructed in and through our discourse, and actions, through praxis. (p. 420)

Thus, according to this point of view, the validity of the present discourse lies in its trustworthiness. Moreover, if validation is reformulated according to Mishler into a social discourse, then the very process of the present work involves at least an attempt at constructing knowledge that in its very nature does not aspire to be free of conflict and controversy.

AMIA LIEBLICH

This book is based on conversations between four female psychologists that took place in Jerusalem in 1990. Since then, a long time has passed, and we have gone our different ways. In the meantime, the tapes of the conversations were transcribed and edited, copies were distributed among the four of us, thoughts and reflections about what we had accomplished were shared on different occasions, and a perspective on the whole project was gained by each of us separately, as well as all of us together, as a group. The long interval between the conception of this book and its birth can be partly accounted for by the fact that it had four mothers. Thus, the process of communicating (back and forth between the United States and Israel, and in Israel, between Jerusalem and Haifa), arguing, deciding, and carrying out our thoughts—grew four times longer than it would have been otherwise. In other words, ongoing conversations characterized the project far beyond the conversations recorded in this volume. Our main argument, however, is that much has been gained in this unique process. The following discussion attempts to explicate this gain.

Our initial aim was to elaborate, in the form of a four-woman conversation, on Josselson's eight dimensions of relating, as experienced by individuals who live (or have lived) in the Israeli kibbutz. This could have been defined as a bilateral goal: to understand the interpersonal aspects of the kibbutz better with the aid of Josselson's theory, and to illuminate the theory, by applying it to the special case of the kibbutz. An edited version of these conversations appears in the preceding chapters. Consequently, the present chapter will be organized around three foci: the process of our joint project, namely conversation as method; the contents of this study, that is, the contribution of Josselson's relational theory for understanding growing up communally; and, finally, the importance of context for theory and research regarding human relationships.

A. Process—Conversation as Method

As one of us said right in the beginning, essentially the process consisted of "putting our heads together" to understand a phenomenon of high complexity in human development and relationships.

I would like to start this discussion with a reflection that may seem inappropriate but has, from my point of view, tremendous relevance. Accidentally or not, Ruthellen started our recorded meetings with a quotation from Martin Buber, from a book called *The Knowledge of Man*, presenting a problem of social relations that arises, according to Buber (1965), "wherever the life of a number of men, living with one another, bound up together, brings in its train shared experiences and reactions" (p. 72). But we are female scholars. The kibbutz membership—our research subjects—consisted of both women and men. And, when talking about relationships, we are often discussing women (not only men) relating to men, children, infants, the elderly, or "just" other women. In other words, what Buber said, in his choice of the terms, excluded us from the discourse, in spite of the fact that women shared or perhaps dominated the kind of experiences that he referred to. The choice of words may have been of no special importance at the time Buber wrote his essay, but reading them today immediately brings up the question of women's place in culture, and "women's ways of knowing" (Belenky, Clinchy, Goldberger, & Tarule, 1986) as probably differing from masculine knowledge or discourse.

This is indeed a central aspect of the "method" we have demonstrated in this book. One of the ways to discuss the process of conversations about theory and research on relationships in the kibbutz, is by presenting it as a feminist research approach (Reinharz, 1992). Using qualitative or narrative research models, collaboration in intellectual endeavor, informal power structure among researchers, and a deep concern for relationship with the research subjects and among researchers—all of these have been characterized as feminist ways of conducting research. I do not think that this is entirely justified, yet it is perhaps true that with the influx of women scholars into the fields of social science and health, a movement away from the strict positivistic paradigm for conducting psychological research has taken place.

Whatever one's opinion on the issue of the feminist contribution to "softer" research approaches in psychology, it has been widely accepted that women's lives evolve in the context of interpersonal relations, perhaps more so than the lives of men (Gilligan, 1982; Miller, 1986). Recently, however, researchers seem to have reached the point that studying women and girls has made us aware of the place of relationships in men's lives as well, while the gender differences are perhaps in the kind or form of relationship rather than their importance or prevalence (Josselson, 1992). If we agree that the use of conversation as a means to elaborate on theory and research, as demonstrated in this book, is a relational method of scholarship, as such, it is perhaps "feminist" or using the force of "women's ways of knowing." It manifests the joint effort of four women, who chose not to write separate papers, or to discuss each other's work in critical reviews, but to sit for hours, face to face, and conduct conversations about their work. I believe that as this last decade of the century approaches its end, men in the social sciences are also drawn more and more toward these methods.

I will now leave the (perhaps irrelevant) question of the significance of feminism in the realm of relational research methods and writing and try to describe the actual process that went into the production of the present book. The four researchers who participated in these conversations have conducted completely separate studies on kibbutz members or ex-members in Israel, as was described in the Introduction.

Bringing our different scholarship to the conversation thus combines different kinds of general expertise (social or developmental psychology, clinical background, etc.), of research approaches, and of periods studied. In addition, although none of us was ever a kibbutz member, we differ in what might be termed our distance from the studied phenomenon. More specifically, Josselson is an American and therefore has a wider comparative perspective on lifestyles and relationships. The other three are Israelis, with more intimate knowledge of the field.

As a result of the four of us getting together for open conversations, coming from our different experiences and perspectives, a common and complex new Gestalt has emerged. Let me start with the style and nature of the individual discourse. As readers probably noticed, each of the speakers brought up her ideas in a fairly informal manner, expressing her point of view and describing examples (mostly prepared beforehand) for the dimension under discussion. The individual speaker's part frequently includes an elaboration of how she has arrived at the statement she is making, questions that have remained open, doubts that she has about what she is saying, free associations that do not appear as completely relevant—all aspects of the "undertext," which usually remain unrevealed in academic writing. It is these parts of the conversation, however, that to my mind are most constructive for a deeper understanding of the topic. They allow readers to become active in learning about the subject, in interpreting or criticizing the proposal or conclusion offered by the speaker, for example.

Following the individual part of the conversation, an interaction with other speakers develops. This may take various conversational forms. At several points in the recorded discourse, a simple question-answer interaction takes place. A speaker may ask: Do you know so and so? or

Do you have such material in your research? A simple answer providing the information is sometimes given, but no less frequent is a response that shares lack of knowledge or conviction on some matters, in a plain "I don't know" answer. The majority of the questions, however, are not for additional information but invite the others to participate in the conversation by bringing in their own opinions and evidence on the matter under discussion. This often happens spontaneously, without posing a question—when the four women freely join the conversation in bringing their associations, reactions, evidence, quotations, and examples, sometimes agreeing and at other times disagreeing with each other. As readers may have noticed, the reactions of "I don't understand this" or "I disagree with you" have been not only legitimate, but highly productive for the continuation of the conversation. Even when disagreeing, a sense of sharing and validation of each other's interests, concerns, conclusions, and intuitions permeates the conversations.

Some of these conversational reactions have the nature of deepening the point—namely, framing the example given in a clearer conceptual mode, providing it with a more profound or richer interpretation, perhaps from clinical experience, or proposing a theoretical term for the phenomenon. Other reactions may be labeled as broadening the point, usually by comparing it to other contexts: for example, comparing the behavior of city children to kibbutz children, or bringing into the conversation theories, formerly published research, and studies by other people as possible contexts for the point being made. Between these two kinds of conversational interaction is a third one, which I will term *elaborating*, when one speaker presents a point, with or without an example, and the others bring additional examples for it from their own research. This creates a collage of sorts, in which examples based on different methodologies, different studied age groups, different periods of time in the history of the kibbutz, and so on, are added by each of the speakers. As a result of these interactions flowing in free conversation, a rich multidimensional picture is gradually created for each of the topics, namely Josselson's eight dimensions of relations. The movement of the conversation seems to be cyclic—presenting an issue, example, question, clarification, another example, and so on—in different orders, of course—and returning to some of the same issues and questions from a higher level of understanding.

As the conversation goes on, the four participants emerge as having different roles and conversational personalities. Ruthellen is the originator of the theory that provides the contents for the discussion. She has the role of an expert on these quite innovative concepts about relational space, and the three others refer to her as such, for example, asking, Does this example fit your concept of eye-to-eye validation or perhaps it belongs to mutuality, which we will discuss later? She often opens and summarizes the conversation on each of the dimensions. In addition, she is an American and therefore sometimes provides a context of cross-cultural perspective, and she is a clinician and therefore willing to provide some deeper interpretations of examples given. Her method of data gathering is unique among the four of us: she is using an original instrument for drawing maps of one's relational space throughout life.

Ruth also uses her clinical experience in framing some of the issues and interpreting instances provided in the conversation. However, her role is definitely that of broadening the discussion again and again. She often supplements the conversation with theoretical conceptions in the areas of either developmental psychology or personality theory. She provides lots of information on other studies or empirical research on growing up in the kibbutz, intimacy in the kibbutz compared with other settings, and so on. She brings up repeatedly the comparative aspect of kibbutz- versus city-raised individuals. She is most acquainted with quantitative data on the kibbutz at present, and most cautious about lack of controlled studies and other methodological issues in the quoted results. Her own studies on the kibbutz were often quantitative, using questionnaire materials for the study of intimacy and friendship.

I have the longest career of studying the kibbutz, from psychological, sociological, and historical perspectives. Often I add the temporal dimension to the conversation, comparing the present situation of the kibbutz with its past, referring to the unique structure of the early kibbutzim, their past aims and goals. Rather than comparing relationships of kibbutz-raised individuals to other cultural contexts, I propose a generational scheme to develop a differential picture of relationships within the kibbutz itself.

Hadas, who is the youngest among the four women, often has the role of an integrator. She integrated the concepts of relational dimensions with her interview studies on loneliness in the kibbutz. She combines in her work both quantitative and qualitative approaches. She has precise examples to provide for each of the dimensions, highly sensitive quotations that she has prepared in advance. She has a fresh view on many of the issues and seems to discover new connections within and between ideas mentioned by others, such as when noticing that the word *chaver*, meaning a kibbutz member, is actually the same word as "friend" in Hebrew. Both she and I know the same corpus of transcripts from our joint research, thus enabling the two of us to refer back and forth to this data. However, while I draw my knowledge from general life stories of kibbutz members or ex- members, Hadas's interviews were more focused on relationships and loneliness in the kibbutz.

Although the foregoing description creates an exaggerated and rigid role division of the four women in the conversation, a lot of flexibility remained in the actual interaction, as demonstrated in the preceding chapters. Yet, the personal input of each woman is different in an often consistent manner, thus adding color and texture to the common discourse. Finally, as the topic that we planned to study is in the realm of relationships, the relationship of the four of us within the context of the conversation, or the interpersonal system created for the purpose of this joint project, is played out clearly for readers to absorb or to judge.

B. Contents—The Dimensions of Interpersonal Space as Applied to Relationships in the Kibbutz

It is possible to evaluate the contents of the conversations from two directions: what have we learned about theory on relationships, and what have we learned about the interpersonal realm of communally raised individuals. The learning process that becomes apparent in the conversations has enriched us in both directions. In terms of Josselson's theory, it was demonstrated that the dimensions differentiate among various aspects of relationships and open new avenues for understanding some of the hidden, silent facets of the relational space. Research by the three Israeli authors, which was not initially planned to test or demonstrate Josselson's theory, proved to gain in meaning and depth when the theory was applied to their findings and examples. The application of the concepts of, for example, holding or idealization, to previously conducted research and to clinical impressions was experienced by us as being both natural and productive. Rather than doing what previous research on the kibbutz tended to do, namely, generalizing and stating that the kibbutz children or adults have more or fewer friendships, are more or less lonely, the eight dimensions deconstructed the totality of such claims and provided a rich and fertile perspective

Reflections on the Discourse 145

for looking at the kibbutz in a fresh manner by focusing separately on each of the dimensions. In fact, what we experienced as still missing in the conversations is the next stage, of integrating the dimensions into various patterns (e.g., a stress on validation with idealization, or the opposite trends of holding and validation, etc.) that may be characteristic of kibbutz- versus city-raised women and men.

Due to the richness of the conversations, both in evidence and theory, it is not easy to summarize the conclusions of the four of us on the eight dimensions in the kibbutz. I will discuss only some highlights here. We seemed to agree that holding is a very strong aspect of the kibbutz relational space, in the sense of having people and a place to fall back on. Individuals spoke about being held securely by the kibbutz community, although for a smaller group, this strong holding was experienced as somewhat suffocating. In spite of the common educational system and early attempts of the kibbutz community to put down family ties, the sense of belonging to one's parents and family, in the form of attachment, was noted as similar for kibbutz members and city people. Being raised communally did not produce higher fear of abandonment among kibbutz members. We discussed parenting, especially motherhood, in this context and noted how rules regarding "good parenting" have changed over time. Beyond family attachment, the kibbutz community can be characterized by the strong attachment within the peer group. This may be interpreted, however, as another manifestation of the holding aspect in the kibbutz.

Eye-to-eye validation was presented as a central dimension to differentiate communally raised individuals, because it seems to be harder to get in the kibbutz society. Since equality and the peer group are highly emphasized in the kibbutz, many interviewees felt that they lacked a sense of uniqueness and had often been psychologically invaded by the commune. Several of them described the painful process of learning who they were only after having left the kibbutz. The other side of the same dimension is experienced as transparency, namely, being known all too well by others, having no private space and no right to be alone, with a related phenomenon of being unable to change a stigma or label attached to oneself. How can individual passion for another be incorporated with loyalty and commitment to the commune? Can passion arise in a group of people who grow up communally, sharing everything? How free is sex among youth in the kibbutz, and is it considered as "love"? Are there real differences in the passion dimension among the kibbutz and nonkibbutz world? Opinions on these matter varied among the speakers, as evidence from various periods in the history of the kibbutz and their own research were shared and discussed among them. There is more agreement among participants in the conversation regarding the area of idealization-identification. Since ideology is such a central aspect of growing and living in a kibbutz, people in the kibbutz—more than in other settings—come to connect to others who represent or embody certain kinds of ideals. Values create deep conflicts among individuals also. First-generation pioneers, or the parents or grandparents generation, are frequently idolized. Ideals and values are so central for the world of relationships in the kibbutz that when ideology fails, or declines, people reported experiencing a sense of loneliness.

The best-friend phenomenon, intimacy between two or more individuals, which is part of the meaning of mutuality, is greatly affected and probably diminished by the demand or norm of togetherness for all. Furthermore, the mechanism of gossip inhibits sharing of secrets, and having the same reality and no distance eliminates the need for it. While people experience companionship and more superficial social connections within the kibbutz, they often tend to find best friends, people with whom they can experience deep disclosure, outside the kibbutz community. On the other hand, embeddedness, defined as finding one's place in a group, belonging to a network larger than the self, is remarkable in the social life of kibbutz members of all ages. As a consequence of the salience of this dimension, people who feel a sense of not belonging—for example, newcomers— feel highly alienated from the society, and people with strong individual needs may have an intense wish to break away from it. The process of absorption of new members and of learning a new language was discussed in the framework of this sense of embeddedness.

The last dimension of Josselson's theory is tenderness and caring, which brought us back to a topic that highly involved us as women, mothers and daughters. The conversation dealt with caregiving in the kibbutz family, common education system, and general society. We discussed professional regulated care versus spontaneous and emotional care, as well as the topic of gender and tenderness, pointing to the history of child-raising practices and how women of the kibbutz reclaimed caring in recent years. Although there were many disagreements among the four of us about specific points regarding this dimension, we all felt that our understanding of the relationships in the kibbutz—and the nature of relational space anywhere—was greatly enhanced by sharing our knowledge and our still open questions.

C. Learning About Context

In psychological theory, the context is often neglected, and broad generalizations are proposed disregarding culture, time, gender, class, and other important variables that differentiate among human beings. Our conversations brought us repeatedly to the realization of the importance of context in everything we said. First of all, a relationship is in itself contextual, as it deals with processes both inside and outside the individual "skin." But above and beyond this basic fact, gathering to talk about relatedness in a kibbutz, a social and geographical system of well-defined boundaries, raised our consciousness to the fact that relationships always occur in a setting. In other words, there seem to be three levels inherent in the psychology of relationships: the individual, the pair or group that relates as individuals, and the context within which this takes place.

Our conversations were often comparative: how do communally raised people relate to each other as compared to individuals raised in noncommunal environments that exist right at their gates and all around them? Has the Israeli, perhaps Jewish, context anything unique to contribute as a broader cultural background in which the phenomena under discussion are embedded? Would a kibbutz in Japan reproduce the same patterns that we observed in our studies? Would it be the same in religious Israeli kibbutzim, which were lightly represented in the research discussed in our conversations? Furthermore, in talking about the kibbutz, which has a short history of less than 100 years, we became aware of the vast differences between past and present in the social life of individual members and the system as a whole. Although its history is short, many major changes have occurred in the kibbutz since its foundation. A gradual relaxation of communal institutions and norms has culminated in the abandonment of common education for infants and younger children, returning sons and daughters (after school hours) to their parents' homes, thus diminishing the centrality of the kibbutz-children peer group and changing the pattern of motherhood and fatherhood. Later on, in the period not yet fully discussed in the conversations, other aspects of the commune have been revoked, as more individual freedom and private property are allowed in the present kibbutzim. How will these changes affect relationships between individuals? In taking account of the historical dimension, a generational scheme was offered. The pioneers were highly idealistic individuals who put their commune above all personal needs. Their children, the second generation, grew up in a very orthodox, communally run educational system. They came to inherit their parents' creation, were awed by them and hesitant about changing anything. But the kibbutz did change under their leadership, and the third generation was raised mostly in the newly introduced family sleeping arrangements, and, as a result, they were more keenly aware of their individuality. How did these three generations fare in creating and maintaining interpersonal relations? Obviously, there will be significant differences here. In recent years, the gender context of relationships has received a lot of attention in psychological and feminist literature. The notion that men and women differ in their relational space as studied by the four of us was, however, fairly marginal in the conversations. Women talked more, perhaps more freely, about their relationship, but undoubtedly men related as much as women did. A much more neglected contextual aspect of relationships is the language in which people define themselves and their relational space and relate to each other in practice. This silent, elusive background factor was seldom touched by our conversations—conversations that took place in English, while the interviews and quotations that most of us brought to the gathering were originally in Hebrew. In the interpersonal domain, as in all other subjects covered by languages, a language develops a terminology that allows for awareness of certain aspects of relationships, on the one hand, and is influenced by cultural, social, and religious qualities of relating that characterize the users of this language throughout time, on the other. The Hebrew word *kibbutz* in itself means the active act of collection together, the collection of people. The word for kibbutz member, *chaver*, means friend. But it is not a naturally flowing friendship, but friendship tested by living in the community and voted on after a long candidacy period. Perhaps other specific aspects of relating in the kibbutz are influenced by the language available for their experience and description. It is essential to take into account these contextual factors in studying how people relate to each other, and try to achieve more specific accounts for differences among human and cultural settings.

Reflections on the Discourse

RUTH SHARABANY

The present methodology used in this book is new, not in process but in regarding the process as a legitimate methodology. The usual scientific model that is common in psychology has been one of carefully carried out experiments or other field studies, with very carefully formulated conclusions based on generalizations that remain close to the data. However, in terms of accumulated knowledge, it is clear that after people read these carefully conducted studies, when they indeed draw their own conclusions, they go beyond the results of the very specific studies and make personal generalizations. Moreover, their subjective interpretations of the studies are used as a stepping stone for making minor or major leaps, to the next hypothesis, theory, or applied issue. For example, experiments in the laboratory on learning conducted with animals were applied to human learning in various ways—first, perhaps as overgeneralizations and then as a source theory and hypothesis that could be studied systematically. The intermediate phase has potential both for being at risk of error and at the same time for being a creative phase that often is not documented as such. It tends to find its place in less formal publications, but without the emphasis on describing the process that led to a particular integration. The process may be detected (or not) by the critical reader. It is this process of joining the pieces of the quilt that is most often hidden and is left not clearly articulated; hence, it is unavailable for scrutiny. These kinds of leaps are made outside scientific, written, and documented studies, and most often are made orally. Another place where this process of drawing applied conclusions from a diverse body of knowledge occurs is in policy-making situations.

The usual scientific process is such that there is a gap between the research phase and the conclusion by the scientific community (and, of course, the public). In the present work, by using a method that presents the discourse, the process of making conclusions and generalizations is explicit and open to criticism and corrections by readers. It is not left implicit and idiosyncratic for readers. This is definitely a strength of the present methodology. However, it also reveals the shortcomings and makes the doubts explicit.

A question may be asked as to how meta-analysis of a large database or any other method of review of a large body of knowledge is different from our discussion in the present book. We think that an important ingredient is the integration of multimethod and multiperspective approaches, particularly the attempt to integrate quantitative and qualitative studies. In most reviews and particularly in the method of meta-analysis, the review is subjected to clear boundaries of methodology. One of the main features of the present discussion was the equal share/status allocated to both qualitative and quantitative methodology. The commitment to give an equal weight to both methodologies is not an easy task. It underscores potential dilemmas and conflicts inherent in the process, beyond those that arise naturally in an attempt to review studies within the same tradition. Currently, we lack tools and criteria by which this integration itself can be evaluated (unlike specific criteria within quantitative methodology, such as effect size, nature of the sample, and so on). In the present work, the discourse was based on a unified framework, which was provided by Ruthellen's conceptualization of the eight dimensions of close relationships. In the process of the discourse, the diversity of the methods (quantitative and qualitative) was then applied systematically to the relatedness dimensions and questions under discussion. The application of the dimensions to data was conducted post hoc, in the sense that we came back to our own data, looking at it through the prism of the relatedness dimensions. For example, in my studies of the kibbutz through the conceptualization of intimacy, the definition of the aspect of holding had not been defined or explicated. Using the relatedness framework produced a new way of looking at the data that required a new examination, leading to fresh ways that enriched the picture of closeness in the kibbutz.

In studying the kibbutz, there is a special aspect of kibbutz subjects that needs to be considered. The kibbutz is unique in that it is closely in touch with research. Subjects tend to be very interested in the findings of studies in which they participate, not only as mere subjects but even more so as a society: a society that is interested in continuing to shape its experimental society into an enlightened, educated, and ideological society.

Since the kibbutz form of life, and especially its form of socialization and child-rearing practices, has been a novel and unique phenomenon, both researchers and kibbutz members have sought to evaluate and compare the benefits and costs of their special way of life, particularly in the educational realm. In many ways, there has been apprehension since there was a danger that any conclusion would carry a unidimensional verdict of good or bad, success or failure, in a way of life.

The kibbutz was, from its very beginning, perceived by social scientists as a unique opportunity to study ecological variations and personality development. Kibbutzniks became accustomed to being subjects, completing questionnaires, and so on. The social and psychological issues studied by both kibbutz researchers and outsiders were very meaningful, and the kibbutz establishment observed them with both anxiety and readiness to draw conclusions relevant to their life on the kibbutz. Studies conducted on the kibbutz, therefore, bore the underlying meaning of being both a reflection on kibbutz life and potentially a source of criticism. Studies were also considered as a form of feedback, input that is relevant to decision making on various rather central and specific aspects of kibbutz life. The kibbutz is a well-educated society, ideologically minded, and very communicative. Thus, research on the kibbutz has been perceived as a source of input for their debates and discussions about their educational system. An issue may be raised as to the best or correct relationship between social investigators and their subjects. The relationship may be anywhere from a correctly distant, objectified position to a very subjective and involved position of a participant-observer. An example is the work of Bettelheim (1969) on the kibbutz, which was criticized as having the shortcomings of an outsider's point of view. Thus, descriptions that were at odds with common attitudes about the kibbutz were then attributed and explained away as stemming from Bettelheim's being outsider both to Israeli society and the kibbutz. In the present discourse, none of us can claim that we live on a kibbutz or are kibbutz members. Three of us, by being Israelis, were close to kibbutz life, spending time on kibbutzim as part of the general Israeli nationalistic education, which sought to adopt values of the kibbutz and has tended to see the kibbutz as a model to be aspired to for the national cause. Kibbutzniks were regarded as the Mayflower pioneers, central to all the national political and military life in Israel.

RUTHELLEN JOSSELSON

In a recent paper (Josselson, 1995), I began to sketch the idea that the critically revealing segment of any interview is the one in which the participant begins to engage in a dialogue with her/himself, the moment when the parts of the self are in conversation, revealing both the multiplicity of the participant's experience and the tensions between these aspects of the self. Reflecting on this long conversation with my colleagues, I begin to wonder if the same isn't true of more general areas of knowledge. Perhaps we can know a field of scholarship best when we can engage those areas of tension where multiple facets of understanding intersect, interweave, collide, contradict, and show themselves in their shifting and often paradoxical relation to each other. This is what I believe we have achieved here. Together we have explored the question of sociocultural influences on human relationships and discovered the diversity that exists among those who had the experience of being raised in an ideologically based communal setting. Inevitably, our talk ferreted out the dilemmas, and we found that we must investigate ever more localized forms (Geertz, 1973)—that it makes a difference what generation the kibbutz member belonged to, who his or her parents were—and that idiosyncratic needs often portended the nature of response each individual had to the experience of communal "family."

As a "foreigner," I felt privileged to have the opportunity to share my observations and insights with those closer to the culture I was trying to understand, with people who could place what I was learning in richer and deeper contexts, who could suggest alternative explanations of what my participants disclosed to me, and who could offer either confirming or disconfirming observations from their own, much more extensive research. As a foreigner, I was also naive to the political implications of concluding one thing or another, and I think that my innocence of this context also brought something to the discussion, moving it more solidly onto conceptual ground. Thus, both knowledge and ignorance had something to offer to this joint effort to construct understanding.

I learned a great deal about relationships from this conversation. Most generally, I came to a deeper understanding of the inevitable enigmas in all relationships, in all social life. There is never a "best way." I never did find it meaningful to wonder if the kibbutzim were "good" or "bad" for relationships. When people come together, there is always a dialectic between togetherness and aloneness, always the twin dangers of merging and isolation. Increasingly, in industrialized cities, we struggle with the problems of people being too much separated from one another, looking out only for themselves. In the kibbutz, we see the

Reflections on the Discourse 153

dilemmas of the other side, the problems attendant to people being multiply interconnected in a context that prizes group membership over individuation.

I am aware of the parallel process at work in this conversation: We studied communal society by creating a communal form of knowing. We explored the ways in which we could put our individual ways of knowing together—and I think we did this in a respectful, mutually enriching way. Like the kibbutz members who formed the subject of our discussion, we put aside our needs for individual recognition in the service of a common purpose. And, like the kibbutz members, we gave birth to a group product; yet each of us carries away a more personal, individual kind of learning.

I believe, with Bakhtin (1986), that all research is fundamentally conversation. What we have done here is to make this explicit and overt. But we are also in dialogue with readers whom we cannot see or hear. We have yet to discover whether or not this is a valuable way for our readers to learn as well.

REFERENCES

Ainsworth, M. D. S., Blehar, M., Waters, E., & Wall, S. (1978). *Patterns of attachment.* Hillsdale, NJ: Lawrence Erlbaum.

Arnon, A. (1978). *Emotional expression and intimate friendship toward significant others in kibbutz with familial and communal sleeping arrangements of preadolescents.* M.A. thesis, University of Tel Aviv (Hebrew).

Avgar, A., Bronfenbrenner, U., & Henderson, C. R., Jr. (1977). Socialization practices of parents, teachers, and peers in Israel: Kibbutz, moshav, and city. *Child Development, 48*, 1219-1227.

Aviezer, O., Van Ijzendoorn, H. M., Sagi, O., & Schuengel, C. (1994). "Children of the dream" revisited: 70 years of collective early child care in Israeli kibbutzim. *Psychological Bulletin, 116*, 99-116.

Bakhtin, M. M. (1986). *Speech genres and other essays.* Austin: University of Texas Press.

Baumeister, R. F., & Newman, L. S. (1994). How stories make sense of personal experiences: Motives that shape autobiographic narratives. *Personality and Social Psychology Bulletin, 20*, 676-690.

Best-Hallahmi, B., & Rabin, A. I. (1977). The kibbutz as a social experiment and as a child-rearing laboratory. *American Psychologist, 32*(7), 532-541.

Belenky, M. F., Clinchy, B. M., Goldberger, N. R., & Tarule, J. M. (1986). *Women's ways of knowing.* New York: Basic Books.

Berman, E. (1988). Communal upbringing in the kibbutz: The allure and risks of psychoanalytic utopianism. *Psychoanalytic Study of the Child, 43*, 319-335.

Bettelheim, B. (1969). *The children of a dream: Communal child-rearing and its implications for society.* New York: Macmillan.

Biran, D. (1983). *Emotional experience and its verbal expression among kibbutz and city adolescents.* M.A. thesis, University of Haifa (Hebrew).

References

Bowlby, J. (1982). *Attachment and loss: Vol. 1.* New York: Basic Books. (Original work published 1969)
Breznitz, S. (1985). Chores as a buffer against risky interaction. *Schizophrenia Bulletin, 11,* 357-359.
Buber, M. (1965). *The knowledge of man.* New York: Harper & Row.
Dana-Engelstein, N. (1978). *Repression-sensitization and interpersonal relationship in kibbutz and moshav.* M.A. thesis, University of Haifa (Hebrew).
Devereux, E. C., Jr., Bronfenbrenner, U., Rodgers, R. R., Kav-Venaki, S., Keily, E., & Karson, E. (1974). Socialization practices of parents, teachers, and peers in Israel: The kibbutz versus the city. *Child Development, 45,* 269-281.
Douvan, E., & Adelson, J. (1966). *The adolescent experience.* New York: John Wiley.
Edelist, M. (1980). *Creativity in the kibbutz.* Master's thesis, Department of Psychology, University of Haifa.
Edry, G. (1995). *Attachment patterns and perception of relationship with parents and peers in kibbutz women from different sleeping arrangements.* M.A. thesis, University of Haifa (Hebrew).
Erikson, E. (1964). *Insight and responsibility.* New York: Norton.
Fox, N. (1977). Attachment of kibbutz infants to mother and metapelet. *Child Development, 48,* 1228-1239.
Fried, Y. (1960). Hitpatchut psychomotoric shel yaldey hakibbutz [Psychomotor development of the kibbutz children]. *Ofakim, 14,* 303-312.
Fuchs, O. (1995). *The relation between help-seeking behavior, attachment style, and lodging style in the kibbutz.* M.A. thesis, University of Haifa.
Geertz, C. (1973). *The interpretation of cultures.* New York: Basic Books.
Gewirtz, J. (1965). The course of infant smiling in four child-rearing environments in Israel. In B. M. Foss (Ed.), *Determinants of infant behavior* (pp. 205-250). London: Methuen.
Gilligan, C. (1982). *In a different voice.* Cambridge, MA: Harvard University Press.
Harlow, H. F., & Harlow, M. (1966). Learning to love. *American Scientist, 54*(3), 44-272.
Harlow, M. (1963). Affection. In D. L. Sills (Ed.), *International encyclopedia of the social sciences* (Vol. 1, pp. 121-125). New York: Macmillan and Free Press.
Hershlag, E. (1984). *Intimacy and reciprocal familiarity of emotions among married couples in the city and in the kibbutz.* Unpublished M.A. thesis, University of Haifa (Hebrew).
Holmes, D. (1989). Informal versus formal supports for impaired elderly people—Determinants of choice in Israeli kibbutzim. *The Gerontologist, 29*(2), 195-202.
Jordan, J. (1986). *The meaning of mutuality* (Work in progress, Stone Center Working Paper Series, No. 23). Wellesley, MA: Stone Center.
Josselson, R. (1992). *The space between us: Exploring the dimensions of human relationships.* San Francisco: Jossey-Bass.
Josselson, R. (1995). Imagining the real: Empathy, narrative, and the dialogic self. In R. Josselson & A. Lieblich (Eds.), *The narrative study of lives: Vol. 3. Interpreting experience.* Thousand Oaks, CA: Sage.
Kaffman, M., Shoham, S., & Elizur, E. (1986). Divorce in the kibbutz: Who is the initiator and why? *Israel Journal of Psychiatry and Relative Science, 23*(3), 169-181.
Kaffman, M., Shoham, S., Palgi, M., & Rosner, M.(1986). Divorce in the kibbutz: Past and present. *Contemporary Family Therapy, 8*(4), 301-315.
Kaminer, H. (1979). *The linkage between socialization and relationships of adults toward their parents: A comparison between kibbutz and moshav.* M.A. thesis, University of Haifa (Hebrew).

Kav-Venaki, S., Levin, I., Esformes, Y., & Karson, E. (1978). Patterns of self and intragroup evaluations in two different Israeli preadolescent peer groups: The kibbutz and the city. *Journal of Cross Cultural Psychology, 9*(2), 237-252.

Kohut, H. (1977). *The restoration of the self*. New York: International Universities Press.

Lev-Ran, A. (1980). *The development of intimate friendship among kibbutz children: A longitudinal study*. M.A. thesis, University of Haifa (Hebrew).

Lieblich, A. (1981). *Kibbutz Makom*. New York: Pantheon.

Lieblich, A. (1989). *Transition to adulthood during military service: The Israeli case*. Albany: State University of New York Press.

·Loevinger, J. (1959). Patterns of parenthood as theories of learning. *Journal of Abnormal & Social Psychology, 59*, 148-150.

Lulav, D. (1994). *Attachment patterns of kibbutz mothers, their attitudes toward raising children, and the adjustment of their children in different sleeping arrangements*. M.A. thesis, University of Haifa (Hebrew).

Maccoby, E. E., & Feldman, S. S. (1972). Mother-attachment and stranger reactions in the third year of life. *Monographs of the Society for Research in Child Development, 37* (1, Serial No. 146).

Main, M., & Goldwyn, R. (1990). *An adult attachment classification system*. Unpublished manuscript, Department of Psychology, University of California, Berkeley.

Miller, J. B. (1986). *What do we mean by relationships?* (Work in progress, Stone Center Working Paper Series, No. 22). Wellesley, MA: Stone Center.

Miller, J. B. (1988). *Connections, disconnections, and violations* (Work in progress, Stone Center Working Paper Series, No. 33). Wellesley, MA: Stone Center.

Mishler, E. G. (1990). Validation in inquiry-guided research: The role of exemplars in narrative studies. *Harvard Educational Review, 60*, 415-442.

Nathan, M., Frenkel, E., & Kugelmass, S. (1993). From adolescence to adulthood: Development of psychopathology in kibbutz and town subjects. *Journal of Youth and Adolescence, 22*(6), 605-621.

Oppenheim, D., Sagi, A., & Lamb, M. E. (1988). Infant-adult attachment on the kibbutz and their relation to socioemotional development 4 years later. *Developmental Psychology, 24*(3), 427-433.

Palgi, M. (1991). Motherhood in the kibbutz. In B. Swirsky & M. P. Safir (Eds.), *Calling the equality bluff* (pp. 261-267). New York: Pergamon.

Peres, Y., & Katz, R. (1980). Stability and centrality: The nuclear family in modern Israel. *Megamot Behavioral Science Quarterly, 26*, 37-55.

Rabin, A. I. (1957). Personality maturity of kibbutz and nonkibbutz children as reflected in Rorschach findings. *Journal of Projective Techniques, 21*, 148-153.

Rabin, A. I., & Best-Hallahmi, B. (1982). *Twenty years later: Kibbutz children grow up*. New York: Springer.

Regev, E. (1976). *Emotional modification and dispersion as a result of communal education in the kibbutz: A comparison between communal sleeping arrangements among kibbutz children and familial sleeping arrangements among city children*. M.A. thesis, University of Haifa (Hebrew).

Regev, E., Best-Hallahmi, B., & Sharabany, R.(1980). Affective expression in kibbutz-communal, kibbutz-familial, and city-raised children. *Child Development, 51*, 232-237.

Reinharz, S. (1992). *Feminist methods in social research*. New York: Oxford University Press.

Rosenthal, L. (1980). *Relations between intimate friendship and peer group orientation in preadolescence*. M.A. thesis, University of Haifa (Hebrew).

References

Rubin, L. (1985). *Just friends: The role of friendship in our lives.* New York: Harper & Row.
Sagi, A., Lamb, M. E., Lewkowicz, K., Shoham, R., Dvir, R., & Estes, D. (1985). Security of infant-mother, -father, and -metapelet attachments among kibbutz-reared Israeli children. In I. Bretherton & E. Waters (Eds.), *Growing points in attachment theory and research.* (Monographs of the Society for Research in Child Development, 50 [1-2, Serial No. 209], 257-275).
Sagi, A., Van Ijzendoorn, M. H., Aviezer, O., Donnell, F., & Mayseless, O. (1994). Sleeping out of home in a kibbutz communal arrangement: It makes a difference for infant-mother attachment. *Child Development, 65,* 992-1004.
Sameroff, A. J., Seifer, R., & Zax, M. (1982). Early development of children at risk for emotional disorder. *Monographs of the Society for Research in Child Development, 47*(7).
Seltzer, V. C. (1989). *The psychological worlds of the adolescent, public and private.* New York: John Wiley.
Shapira, A. (1976). Developmental differences in competitive behavior of kibbutz and city children in Israel. *Journal of Social Psychology, 98,* 19-26.
Sharabany, R. (1974). Intimate friendship among kibbutzim and city children and its measurement (Doctoral dissertation, Cornell University). *Dissertation Abstracts International, 35*(2), 1028b.
Sharabany, R. (1982). Comradeship: Peer group relations among preadolescents in kibbutz vs. city. *Personality & Social Psychology Bulletin, 8,* 302-309.
Sharabany, R. (1994a). Continuities in the development of intimate friendships: Object relations, interpersonal, and attachment perspectives. In R. Erber & R. Gilmour (Eds.), *Theoretical frameworks for personal relationships.* Hillsdale, NJ: Lawrence Erlbaum.
Sharabany, R. (1994b). Intimate friendship scale: Conceptual underpinnings, psychometric properties, and construct validity. *Journal of Social and Personal Relationships, 11,* 449-469.
Sharabany, R., & Hertz-Lazarowitz, R. (1981). Do friends share and communicate more than nonfriends? *International Journal of Behavioral Development, 4,* 45-59.
Sharabany, R., & Rosenthal, L. (1984). Intimacy vs. comradeship: Relationships to best friend compared to group orientation in the Israeli kibbutz. *International Psychology, 40,* 3-21.
Sharabany, R., & Wiseman, H. (1993). Close relationships in adolescence: The case of the kibbutz. *Journal of Youth and Adolescence, 22,* 671-695.
Sharabany, R., & Wiseman, H. (in press). The ecology of growing up with peers in the kibbutz: Research on intimacy, self-disclosure, and emotional expression. In Y. Dar (Ed.), *Kibbutz education in the '90s: Sociological and psychological aspects.* Jerusalem: Academon (Hebrew).
Shepher, J. (1971). *Self-imposed avoidance and exogamy in second-generation kibbutz adults.* Doctoral dissertation, Rutgers University, Department of Anthropology (University Microfilms, Ann Arbor, MI, No. 72-871).
Shouval, R., Kav-Venaki, S., Bronfenbrenner, U., Devereux, E. C., & Kiely, E. (1975). Anomalous reactions to social pressure of Israeli and Soviet children raised in family versus collective settings. *Journal of Personality and Social Psychology, 32*(3), 477-489.
Sobol, J. (1977). *Leil Haessrim* [Hebrew]. Tel Aviv: Bamaagal.
Spiro, M. E. (1958). *Children of the kibbutz.* Cambridge, MA: Harvard University Press.
Strauss, A., & Corbin, J. (1990). *Basics of qualitative research.* Newbury Park, CA: Sage.

Sullivan, H. S. (1953). *The interpersonal theory of psychiatry*. New York: Norton.
Surrey, J. (1987). *Relationship and empowerment* (Work in progress, Stone Center Working Paper Series, No. 13). Wellesley, MA: Stone Center.
Swirski, B., & Safir, M. P. (Eds.). (1991). *Calling the equality bluff*. New York: Pergamon.
Talmon-Garber, Y. (1972). *Family and community in the kibbutz*. Cambridge, MA: Harvard University Press.
Teresi, J. (1989). Factors relating to institutional risk among elderly members of Israeli kibbutzim. *The Gerontologist, 29*(2), 203-208.
Tiger, L., & Shepher, J. (1975). *Women in the kibbutz*. New York: Harcourt Brace Jovanovich.
Toren, Z. (1979). *Developmental changes in the effect of parental discipline and socialization pattern on moral judgment*. M.A. thesis, University of Tel Aviv (Hebrew).
Tzur, M. (1988). *Kehiliatenu* [Our community]. Jerusalem: Yad Ben Zvi.
Wheeler, L., Reis, H., & Nezlek, J. (1983). Loneliness, social interaction, and sex roles. *Journal of Personality and Social Psychology, 45*, 943-953.
Winnicott, D. W. (1958). The capacity to be alone. In D. W. Winnicott (Ed.), *The maturational processes and the facilitating environment* (pp. 29-36). London: The Hogarth Press and the Institute of Psychoanalysis.
Winnicott, D. W. (1965). *The family and individual development*. New York: Basic Books.
Wiseman, H., & Lieblich, A. (1992). Individuation in a collective community. *Adolescent Psychiatry, 18*, 156-179.
Yariv, E. (1983). *Intimacy among adolescent girls with their parents and best friend in kibbutz with communal vs. familial sleeping arrangements*. M.A. thesis, University of Haifa (Hebrew).

INDEX

Acceptance, 76-77
Actualization, 90
Adelson, J., 107
Adolescents:
    attachment, 53, 116-117
    embeddedness, 116-117
    emotional expression, 6-7
    passion among, 62, 63-64, 66-67
    See also Children; Peer groups
Ainsworth, M., 6, 44
Alienation:
    and embeddedness, 115-116, 146
    and tending/care, 124
Ambivalent attachment, 6, 44
Annihilation, 73
Arnon, A., 6, 10, 104
Attachment:
    adolescents, 53, 116-117
    ambivalent, 6, 44
    and embeddedness, 116-117
    and holding environment, 33, 34, 40-41, 145
    and Judaism, 45-46
    and parental pathology, 50-51
    and relationship model, 14, 15
    and sleeping arrangements, 48, 49, 55-56
    and tending/care, 131
    avoidant, 44
    city versus kibbutz child rearing, 43-44, 45
    environmental versus parental, 33, 34, 40
    female experience of, 46-50, 52
    infants, 6, 49
    insecure, 6, 44
    male experience of, 46, 49, 52, 55-56
    multigenerational aspect, 45-46, 47
    myths regarding, 43-44
    peer groups, 54-55, 57
    restrictions in child care, 46-50
    sense of belonging, 45, 51-52
    strange situation, 6, 44-45
    throughout life cycle, 45, 50-51, 53-56
    to fathers, 52, 55
    to metapelet, 51-52
    See also Embeddedness; Holding environment; Idealization/identification; Mutuality/resonance; Passions; Tending/care; Validation, eye-to-eye
Avgar, A., 5

Aviezer, O., 6, 44
Avoidant attachment, 44

Bakhtin, M., 153
Baumeister, R., 137
Belenky, M., 140
Belonging:
    and attachment, 45, 51-52
    and embeddedness, 113-115, 119-121, 146
Berman, E., 3
Best friends:
    and holding environment, 34, 37, 39
    female experience of, 39, 108
    male experience of, 37, 39, 55
    of children, 6, 34, 108
    See also Mutuality/resonance
Best-Hallahmi, B., 2, 3, 11, 46, 69, 109
Bettelheim, B., 2, 3, 43, 54, 76, 123, 151
Biran, D., 7
Blehar, M., 6
Boundaries, 105-106, 109, 111
Bowlby, J., 6, 15, 44
Breznitz, S., 50
Bronfenbrenner, U., 5, 10
Buber, M., 22, 115, 139

Children:
    and idealization/identification, 91-93, 95, 96-97, 98-99
    and incest, 62-63
    and metapelet, 2, 5, 51-52, 124-126, 133
    and mutuality/resonance, 101-102, 103, 104, 107, 108, 109, 110
    and tending/care, 123-128, 133
    best friends of, 6, 34, 108
    cooperation of, 33-34, 37
    discipline of, 5
    education of, 85-86
    effects of communal living, 2-3, 5-8
    experience of sleeping arrangements, 6, 7, 8, 32-33, 36-37, 48, 49, 55-56, 74
    hospitalism syndrome, 5
    in nuclear families, 1-2, 6, 7
    maternal deprivation, 5
    maternal substitution, 5
    of kibbutz leaders, 38
    older children as models, 95
    passion among, 62-64
    restrictions in child care, 46-50
    validation of, 73-80, 81, 82-86
    See also Adolescents; Attachment; Peer groups
Clinchy, B., 140
Co-dependence, 13
Compartmentalization, 119
Comradeship, 104
Cooperation:
    among peer groups, 34
    in holding environment, 33-34, 37-38
    of children, 33-34, 37
Corbin, J., 137
Creativity, 85-86
Cultural aspect, 147-148
    of embeddedness, 113-114, 120-121
    of tending/care, 132-134

Dana-Engelstein, N., 11
Death, 127
Dependence, 13
Devereux, E., 5, 104
Discipline, 5
Discourse methodology:
    and relationship model, 8, 136-137, 139, 144-147, 150
    context sensitivity in, 137, 147-148, 150-151
    elaboration in, 142
    feminist approach, vii-viii, 139-141
    goals, 135, 139
    individual contribution, viii, 9-11, 27, 141, 142-144, 151-153
    participant interaction, 136, 138-139, 141-144
    reliability, 138
    use of narratives, 137
    validity, 138
    versus traditional modes, 135-136, 149-150
Divorce, 7, 68-71
Donnell, F., 6
Douvan, E., 107

Edelist, M., 85
Edry, G., 11

Index

Education, 85-86
Elderly:
    and holding environment, 33-34
    tending/care of, 7-8, 126-130
Elizur, E., 7
Embeddedness:
    and adolescent attachment, 116-117
    and alienation, 115-116, 146
    and communal ideology, 114-115
    and continuity, 117-119
    and individualism, 114, 115, 121
    and kibbutz holidays, 114, 115
    and passion, 68
    and relationship model, 14, 17-18
    and static relationships, 116
    and tending/care, 133-134
    cultural aspect, 113-114, 120-121
    multigenerational aspect, 119
    sense of belonging, 113-115, 119-121, 146
    versus compartmentalization, 119
    See also Attachment; Holding environment; Idealization/identification; Mutuality/resonance; Passions; Tending/care; Validation, eye-to-eye
Emin, 96
Emotional expression:
    adolescents, 6-7
    and validation, 74-75, 76-77
Empathy, 74-75
Esformes, Y., 83
Exclusivity (of couples), 23-24, 60-61, 67-68

Fatherhood, 4
    and attachment, 52, 55
    and idealization/identification, 95, 98
    tending/care, 128-129
    validation of children, 76
    See also Male experience of communal living
Feldman, S., 6
Female experience of communal living:
    attachment, 46-50, 52
    being single, 34-35
    best friends, 39, 108
    idealization/identification, 94, 96-97, 98
    lesbianism, 64
    motherhood, 2, 5, 6, 46-50, 49, 61, 84-85, 123
    mutuality/resonance, 25-27, 102-103, 107, 108, 109, 110-111, 148
    passion, 25-27, 59, 63-64, 65, 70-71
    sleeping arrangements, 49
    tending/care, 123-126, 131-132, 133, 146
    validation, 78-80
Feminism:
    and language, 13, 19n1
    and research, vii-viii, 139-141
Fox, N., 6
Frenkel, E., 3, 50
Fried, Y., 5
Fuchs, O., 11

Geertz, C., 152
Gender differences. *See* Female experience of communal living; Male experience of communal living
Gewirtz, J., 5
Gilligan, C., 25, 140
Goldberger, N., 140
Goldwyn, R., 37

Hamula (clan), 45-46
Harlow, H., 57
Harlow, M., 57
Henderson, C., 5
Hershlag, E., 7
Hertz-Lazarowitz, R., 107
Holding environment:
    and relationship model, 14, 15
    attachment, 33, 34, 40-41, 145
    being single, 34-35
    best friends, 34, 37, 39
    cooperation in, 33-34, 37-38
    dichotomy of, 32, 34-36, 39-40
    elderly, 33-34
    idealization of, 37, 39-40
    independence in, 32, 35, 40-41
    mutuality/resonance, 104

negative experience of, 32, 34-36, 39-40
peer groups, 32-33, 145
restriction of, 32, 35-36, 40-41
security in, 31-36, 40, 56-57, 145
sleeping arrangements, 32-33, 36-37
validation in, 36, 87
See also Attachment; Embeddedness; Idealization/identification; Mutuality/resonance; Passions; Tending/care; Validation, eye-to-eye
Holidays, 4, 114, 115
Holmes, D., 8

Idealization/identification:
actualization, 90
and loneliness, 97, 146
and relationship model, 14, 16-17
and suicide, 90
children, 91-93, 95, 96-97, 98-99
communal ideology, 89, 93-95, 96-98
experience to support idealization, 37, 39-40, 53
fatherhood, 95, 98
female experience of, 94, 96-97, 98
holding environment, 37, 39-40
leadership in, 89-92
male experience of, 93-95, 97, 98
multigenerational aspect, 89-93, 96-97, 98-99, 146
older children as models, 95
religion, 95-96, 99
See also Attachment; Embeddedness; Holding environment; Mutuality/resonance; Passions; Tending/care; Validation, eye-to-eye
Illness, 49, 127, 129, 130, 131-132
Incest, 62-63
Independence, 32, 35, 40-41
Individualism:
and embeddedness, 114, 115, 121
and validation, 73-74, 76-82, 83-87, 108, 145
Infants:
attachment, 6, 49
care of, 2, 6, 49, 61, 84-85, 123

personal versus communal relationship with, 61
Insecure attachment, 6, 44

Jordan, J., 17
Josselson, R., 14, 27, 28, 136, 140, 151
Judaism, 45-46, 147
Just Friends (Rubin), 37

Kaffman, M., 7, 68
Kaminer, H., 11
Karson, E., 83
Katz, R., 46
Kav-Venaki, S., 83
Kibbutz ideology, 4, 21-25
embeddedness, 114-115
tending/care, 124-127, 129-130, 132-134, 146
validation, 84-85
See also Idealization/identification
Kibbutz living:
candidacy in, 114
compartmentalization, 119
cultural aspect, 113-114, 120-121, 132-134, 147-148
effects on children, 2-3, 5-8
holidays, 4, 114, 115
hospitalism syndrome, 5
leadership, 38, 59, 60, 61, 71, 89-92, 148
metapelet, 2, 5, 51-52, 124-126, 133
outside relationships, 106-108, 111-112, 146
religious influences, 45-46, 95-96, 99, 132-133, 147
versus nuclear family, 1-2, 6, 7
See also Female experience of communal living; Male experience of communal living; Multigenerational aspect (of kibbutz); Relationships; Sleeping arrangements
Kibbutz Makom (Lieblich), 9, 25, 34, 136
Knowledge of Man, The (Buber), 22, 139-140
Kohut, H., 17
Kugelmas, S., 3, 50

Index

Labeling, 75-76, 82-83, 86-87, 145
Labor, 90
Lamb, M., 6
Leadership, 148
    children of leaders, 38
    idealization/identification, 89-92
    views on passion, 59, 60, 61, 71
    See also Multigenerational aspect (of kibbutz)
Lesbianism, 64
Levin, I., 83
Lev-Ran, A., 10
Lieblich, A., 9, 11, 53, 136
Loevinger, J., 92
Loneliness:
    ability to be alone, 80-81
    and idealization/identification, 97, 146
    and mutuality/resonance, 105-106, 112
    from sleeping arrangements, 36-37
Lulav, D., 11

Maccoby, E., 6
Main, M., 37, 44
Makom kibbutz, 35-36, 47, 113
Male experience of communal living:
    attachment, 46, 49, 52, 55-56
    best friends, 37, 39, 55
    fatherhood, 4, 52, 55, 76, 95, 98, 128-129
    idealization/identification, 93-95, 97, 98
    mutuality/resonance, 25-27, 107-108, 110-111, 148
    passion, 25-27, 59, 70-71
    sleeping arrangements, 49
    tending/care, 128-129
    validation, 76
Marriage, 7, 60, 61-62, 66, 68-71
Mayseless, O., 6
Metapelet:
    attachment, 51-52
    discipline, 5
    tending/care, 2, 124-126, 133
Miller, J., 17, 140
Mishler, E., 138
Moshav living, 5
Motherhood:
    infant care, 2, 6, 49, 61, 84-85, 123
    maternal deprivation, 5
    maternal substitution, 5
    restrictions in child care, 46-50
    See also Female experience of communal living; Tending/care
Multigenerational aspect (of kibbutz), 147-148
    attachment, 45-46, 47
    care of elderly, 7-8, 33-34, 126-130
    embeddedness, 119
    idealization/identification, 89-93, 96-97, 98-99, 146
Mutuality/resonance:
    and loneliness, 105-106, 112
    and relationship model, 14, 17
    and trust, 108, 109
    boundaries, 105-106, 109, 111
    children, 101-102, 103, 104, 107, 108, 109, 110
    comradeship, 104
    female experience of, 25-27, 102-103, 107, 108, 109, 110-111, 148
    holding environment, 104
    intimate relationship development, 101, 102-105, 106-112
    male experience of, 25-27, 107-108, 110-111, 148
    outside relationships, 106-108, 111-112, 146
    peer groups, 104
    personal space, 101-102, 105-106, 110-111
    sharing information, 105-106, 146
    volunteers impact on, 111-112
    See also Attachment; Embeddedness; Holding environment; Idealization/identification; Passions; Tending/care; Validation, eye-to-eye

Nathan, M., 3, 50
Newman, L., 137
Nezlek, J., 26

Oppenheim, D., 6
Outsiders, 106-108, 111-112, 146

Palgi, M., 23, 68
Passions:
adolescents, 62, 63-64, 66-67
and divorce, 7, 68-71
and egalitarianism, 60-61
and embeddedness, 68
and relationship model, 14, 15-16
children, 62-64
couple exclusivity, 23-24, 60-61, 67-68
extramarital sex, 66, 68, 70-71
female experience of, 25-27, 59, 63-64, 65, 70-71
incest, 62-63
leadership views on, 59, 60, 61, 71
lesbianism, 64
male experience of, 25-27, 59, 70-71
marriage, 7, 60, 61-62, 66, 68-71
personal versus communal commitment, 59, 68
sex regulation, 60, 61-62, 63-64, 65-66
within peer groups, 61-62
See also Attachment; Embeddedness; Holding environment; Idealization/identification; Mutuality/resonance; Tending/care; Validation, eye-to-eye
Peer groups:
attachment, 54-55, 57
cooperation among, 34
holding environment, 32-33, 145
mutuality/resonance, 104
passion among, 61-62
security from, 32-33
sleeping arrangements, 32-33
validation, 83, 84, 145
See also Adolescents; Children
Peres, Y., 46
Personal space, 101-102, 105-106, 110-111
Polish, 113-114

Rabin, A., 2, 3, 11, 46, 69, 109
Regev, E., 3, 10, 74
Reinharz, S., vii, 140
Reis, H., 26
Rejection, 73
Relational space, 14
Relationship model:
and discourse methodology, 8, 136-137, 139, 144-147, 150

and language, 13, 19n1
co-dependence, 13
dependence, 13
dimensions of, 14-19, 28-30
relational space, 14
See also Attachment; Embeddedness; Holding environment; Idealization/identification; Mutuality/resonance; Passions; Tending/care; Validation, eye-to-eye
Relationships:
ability to be alone, 80-81
acceptance, 76-77
alienation, 115-116, 124, 146
annihilation, 73
best friends, 6, 34, 37, 39, 55, 108
boundaries, 105-106, 109, 111
co-dependence, 13
compartmentalization, 119
comradeship, 104
cooperation, 33-34, 37-38
couple exclusivity, 23-24, 60-61, 67-68
dependence, 13
divorce, 7, 68-71
incest, 62-63
independence, 32, 35, 40-41
internalization of, 39-40
intimacy development, 101, 102-105, 106-112
lesbianism, 64
loneliness, 36-37, 97, 105-106, 112, 146
marriage, 7, 60, 61-62, 66, 68-71
outside of kibbutz, 106-108, 111-112, 146
personal space, 101-102, 105-106, 110-111
rejection, 73
sense of belonging, 45, 51-52, 113-115, 119-121, 146
sharing information, 105-106, 146
static, 116
strange situation, 6, 44-45
transparency, 73, 79, 145
trust, 108, 109
versus being single, 34-35
with metapelet, 2, 5, 51-52, 124-126, 133
See also Individualism; Multigenerational aspect

Index

(of kibbutz); Peer groups; Relationship model
Religion:
  and idealization/identification, 95-96, 99
  and tending/care, 132-133
  Judaism, 45-46, 147
Research:
  and language, 13, 19n1
  feminist, vii-viii, 139-141
  See also Discourse methodology; Relationship model
Restriction:
  in child care, 46-50
  of holding environment, 32, 35-36, 40-41
Rosenthal, L., 11, 55
Rosner, M., 68
Rubin, L., 37

Safir, M., 4
Sagi, A., 6, 44
Sameroff, A., 51
Schuengel, C., 44
Security:
  environmental versus parental, 33, 34, 40
  from peer groups, 32-33
  holding environment, 31-36, 40, 56-57, 145
  in sleeping arrangements, 32-33
Seifer, R., 51
Seltzer, V., 84
Sexual activity. See Passions
Shapira, A., 34
Sharabany, R., 3, 6, 10, 34, 55, 107, 108
Shepher, J., 61, 62
Shoham, S., 7, 68
Shomer HaTsair kibbutz, 37, 46, 67
Sleeping arrangements:
  attachment, 48, 49, 55-56
  children's experience of, 6, 7, 8, 32-33, 36-37, 48, 49, 55-56, 74
  female experience of, 49
  holding environment, 32-33, 36-37
  loneliness, 36-37
  male experience of, 49
  peer groups, 32-33
  security in, 32-33

tending/care, 123
Sobol, J., 24
Space Between Us, The (Josselson), 136
Spiro, M., 5, 43
Strange situation, 6, 44-45
Strauss, A., 137
Suicide, 90
Sullivan, H., 53
Surrey, J., 17
Swirsky, B., 4

Talmon-Garber, Y., 4
Tarule, J., 140
Tending/care:
  alienation, 124
  and death, 127
  and relationship model, 14, 18
  and sleeping arrangements, 123
  attachment, 131
  children, 123-128, 133
  communal ideology of, 124-127, 129-130, 132-134, 146
  cultural aspect, 132-134
  elderly, 7-8, 126-130
  embeddedness, 133-134
  female experience of, 123-126, 131-132, 133, 146
  illness, 49, 127, 129, 130, 131-132
  infants, 2, 6, 49, 61, 84-85, 123
  male experience of, 128-129
  metapelet, 2, 124-126, 133
  religious aspect, 132-133
  sense of family, 126-128, 130-133
  See also Attachment; Embeddedness; Holding environment; Idealization/identification; Mutuality/resonance; Passions; Validation, eye-to-eye
Teresi, J., 8
Tiger, L., 62
Toren, Z., 10
Transparency, 73, 79, 145
Trust, 108, 109
Tzur, M., 24, 59

Validation, eye-to-eye:
  ability to be alone, 80-81

acceptance versus nonacceptance, 76-77
and communal ideology, 84-85
and creativity, 85-86
and relationship model, 14, 16
children, 73-80, 81, 82-86
emotional expression, 74-75, 76-77
empathy, 74-75
fathers, 76
female experience of, 78-80
holding environment, 36, 87
individualism, 73-74, 76-82, 83-87, 108, 145
labeling, 75-76, 82-83, 86-87, 145
peer groups, 83, 84, 145
transparency, 73, 79, 145
versus annihilation/rejection, 73
See also Attachment; Embeddedness; Holding environment; Idealization/identification; Mutuality/resonance; Passions; Tending/care
"Validation in Inquiry-Guided Research" (Mishler), 138
Van Ijzendoorn, M., 6, 44

Wall, S., 6
Waters, E., 6
Wheeler, L., 26
Winnicott, D., 15, 16, 80
Wiseman, H., 6, 9, 11

Yariv, E., 10

Zax, M., 51

ABOUT THE AUTHORS

Ruthellen Josselson is Professor of Psychology at Towson State University and on the faculty of The Fielding Institute. Recipient of the APA Henry A. Murray Award (1994) and a Fulbright Research Fellowship (1980-1990), she has also recently been Visiting Professor at the Harvard Graduate School of Education and Forchheimer Professor of Psychology at the Hebrew University in Jerusalem. She is author of *Revising Herself: The Story of Women's Identity From College to Midlife* and *The Space Between Us: Exploring the Dimensions of Human Relationships*. She is also a practicing psychotherapist.

Amia Lieblich is Professor of Psychology at the Hebrew University of Jerusalem, where she served as chairperson from 1982 to 1985. Her books have presented an oral history of Israeli society, dealing with war, POWs, military service, and the kibbutz. Recently, she has published two psychobiographies of female writers: *Conversations With Dvora* (about Dvora Baron) and *Towards Lea* (about Lea Goldberg).

Ruth Sharabany is Associate Professor in the Department of Psychology, University of Haifa, Israel, current chairperson of the department's PhD program, and past chairperson of the Clinical program. She is on the editorial board of the journal *Personal Relations*, of the International Society for the Study of Personal Relationships, and of *Psychology*, the journal of the Israeli Psychological Association. Her PhD is from Cornell University. She was a postdoctoral fellow in developmental research at E.T.S., Princeton, NJ. She taught at Tel Aviv University and was a Visiting Scholar at Macquarie University, Australia, and the University of California at Berkeley. Her current research is on social development, close relationships, and the socialization process.

Hadas Wiseman is Assistant Professor in the School of Education, University of Haifa, Israel, and a registered clinical psychologist in private practice in Tivon. After receiving her PhD from York University, Toronto, Canada, she was a Lady Davis postdoctoral fellow at the Hebrew University of Jerusalem. Her current research interests include interpersonal patterns, loneliness, and psychotherapy research; her work combines quantitative and narrative methodologies.